COSMETOLOGY

PRACTICAL CAREER GUIDES

Series Editor: Kezia Endsley

Computer Game Development & Animation, by Tracy Brown Hamilton
Craft Artists, by Marcia Santore
Culinary Arts, by Tracy Brown Hamilton
Dental Assistants and Hygienists, by Kezia Endsley
Education Professionals, by Kezia Endsley
Fine Artists, by Marcia Santore
First Responders, by Kezia Endsley
Health and Fitness Professionals, by Kezia Endsley
Information Technology (IT) Professionals, by Erik Dafforn
Medical Office Professionals, by Marcia Santore
Nursing Professionals, by Kezia Endsley
Plumbers, by Marcia Santore
Skilled Trade Professionals, by Corbin Collins
Veterinary Technicians and Assistants, by Kezia Endsley
Cosmetology: A Practical Career Guide, by Tracy Brown Hamilton

COSMETOLOGY

A Practical Career Guide

TRACY BROWN HAMILTON

ROWMAN & LITTLEFIELD
Lanham • Boulder • New York • London

Published by Rowman & Littlefield
An imprint of The Rowman & Littlefield Publishing Group, Inc.
4501 Forbes Boulevard, Suite 200, Lanham, Maryland 20706
www.rowman.com

6 Tinworth Street, London SE11 5AL, United Kingdom

British Library Cataloguing in Publication Information Available

Library of Congress Control Number: 2020945797

ISBN 978-1-5381-4475-6 (pbk. : alk. paper)
ISBN 978-1-5381-4476-3 (electronic)

♾™ The paper used in this publication meets the minimum requirements of American
National Standard for Information Sciences—Permanence of Paper for Printed Library
Materials, ANSI/NISO Z39.48-1992.

Contents

Introduction

Welcome to Cosmetology

*W*elcome to the exciting field of cosmetology! This book is the ideal start for understanding the various careers available to you within the cosmetology industry: what is right for you, and what path you should follow to ensure you have all the training, education, and experience needed to succeed in your future career goals.

The field of cosmetology is an exciting one, well suited to anyone who enjoys connecting with people, using their creativity, and helping others look and feel their best. There are many roles and activities that fit under the category of "cosmetology," from hairstylist to makeup artist, from nail treatments to overall health and beauty care. Having so many paths to choose from is exciting, but it can also make it difficult to choose which will be the most fitting to you—but that's just what this book is going to help you do.

A Career in the Cosmetology Industry

Covering every career path involved in the beauty-related industry is beyond the scope of this book. We will however cover the most common, including

- hairstylist
- nail technician
- salon or spa manager
- beautician
- wedding and event stylist
- makeup artist
- skin-care specialist

These jobs are widely available all over the country. Everywhere you go, people are looking for stylists for everyday life as well as special occasions such as weddings. Makeup artists can work for the general population, photo studios, or even the theater. No matter where you live, there will be people who want to look and feel their best, and for that, they will rely on talented, creative, and knowledgeable professionals who know how to really listen to what their clients want.

The good news is the industry is booming: employment for hairstylists and cosmetologists is projected to grow 8 percent from 2018 to 2028.[1] That's faster than the average for all careers in the United States. And not all of these jobs necessarily require that you have a college degree. Population growth is also expected to boost the demand for hair care and other cosmetology-related services. So that's all good news for the aspiring cosmetologist. With this healthy outlook, the future looks bright, as you'll see in the following section.

The Market Today

How does the job market look for young people seeking to enter the field of cosmetology? In a word, it looks quite strong. It is a field that not only offers you flexibility as far as work schedule and where you live but also provides a broad range of possibilities regarding the type of work you will do. And most important, the demand for professional cosmetology services appears to be on the rise, despite economic downturns, across the United States and elsewhere. As long as the customer demand is there, the job security and career outlook for cosmetologists will remain strong.

In addition, turnover of professionals in the industry will make room for younger, newer cosmetologists to enter the workforce. According to the Bureau of Labor Statistics (BLS), a large number of job openings will stem from the need to replace workers who transfer to other occupations, retire, or leave for other reasons.[2]

Keep in mind, despite the high demand, the cosmetology field is a very competitive one. Whether you want to launch your own business or work for a high-profile salon, you will be competing with many other talented, creative, and driven hairstylists and cosmetologists. This book will help you stand out against the large pool of competition and arrive at the career you want.

Unfortunately, the COVID-19 pandemic has had an impact on many of the ways in which we study, work, and generally live. At the onset of the crisis, in many areas of the world, businesses providing cosmetology services to clients—from manicurists to hairdressers—were forced to close to protect both workers and the public from exposure to the virus that causes COVID-19. Because every state as well as every country has different policies related to the virus, in some areas these businesses are reopening at the time of writing—but even in such instances, life and work have not gone back to normal. Restrictions covering what services can be provided and rules related to protection of people—for example, the required use of face masks or a ban on using hair dryers—are strict and may be around for a long time to come. However, the good news is that people will always need hairstylists and cosmetologists. You just need to be flexible and be sure to protect yourself and your clients as you develop your career and build your clientele in this "post-COVID" world.

A career in the cosmetology industry offers a broad range of creative and diverse roles.
GETTY IMAGES/JACOBLUND.

Although people all over the country, from small towns to bustling metropolises, create high demand for cosmetology services, there are some areas where, statistically, cosmetology thrives more than others. The following lists the top twenty best places for hairdressers, hairstylists, and cosmetologists in the United States, according to USA Wage,[3] including average annual salary for 2020 and average starting salary for the same year.

Table 1. Twenty Highest-paying Cities/Areas for Hairdressers, Hairstylists, and Cosmetologists in the United States in 2020

		Average Annual Salary	Entry-level Salary	Employment Number
1	Boulder, Colorado	$47,700	$23,460	650
2	Longview, Washington	$45,690	$27,520	150
3	Wenatchee–East Wenatchee, Washington	$45,370	$25,670	70
4	Casper, Wyoming	$44,440	$29,240	110
5	Eastern North Dakota nonmetropolitan area, North Dakota	$43,910	$17,440	110
6	Worcester, Massachusetts	$42,390	$24,970	630
7	Central Nebraska nonmetropolitan area, Nebraska	$41,900	$20,090	150
8	Seattle-Tacoma-Bellevue, Washington	$40,790	$25,810	6,220
9	Nantucket Island and Marthas Vineyard nonmetropolitan area, Massachusetts	$39,690	$28,070	40
10	Framingham, Massachusetts	$39,410	$22,900	610
11	Cheyenne, Wyoming	$39,400	$17,980	90
12	Bremerton-Silverdale, Washington	$38,430	$30,350	370
13	Northwestern Texas nonmetropolitan area, Texas	$38,050	$26,400	n/a
14	Northwestern Washington nonmetropolitan area, Washington	$37,880	$24,560	150
15	Massachusetts nonmetropolitan area, Massachusetts	$37,860	$25,020	110
16	Boston-Cambridge-Quincy, Massachusetts	$37,340	$24,980	8,520
17	Barnstable Town, Massachusetts	$37,260	$25,270	580
18	Western Colorado nonmetropolitan area, Colorado	$37,060	$33,520	90
19	Western Washington nonmetropolitan area, Washington	$36,910	$26,190	110
20	Mount Vernon–Anacortes, Washington	$36,880	$26,030	200

Source: USA Wage, "Highest-paying Cities for Hairdressers, Hairstylists, and Cosmetologists," www.usawage.com/high-pay/cities-hairdressers_hairstylists_and_cosmetologists.php.

But if you don't live near these cities or don't see yourself wanting to in the future, don't despair! The services you will provide will be in demand wherever you live, and this demand is only projected to grow.

Note: Choosing a specialization will also give you an edge in your career. Cosmetologists who develop an expertise in techniques like hair straightening or coloring will experience an even greater demand for their services, and skin-care specialists are expected to see a growth rate of 11 percent over the next decade—must faster than average, according to the BLS.[4]

What Does This Book Cover?

This book covers the following topics as well as others:

- how to find the kind of job that best suits your personality and preference for working conditions, hours, educational requirements, work culture, and atmosphere. You will learn the day-to-day activities involved in each job and what a typical day at work will look like.
- how to form a career plan—starting now, wherever you are in your education—and how to start taking the steps that will best lead to success
- how to discover and fulfill the educational requirements and opportunities of your chosen career
- how to write your resume, interview, network, and apply for jobs
- how to use all your available resources for further information

"You have to have a strong work ethic and you must have patience. Many spas and salons will start you off as an assistant. It's not very glamorous but it's the stepping-stone for every successful hairdresser."—Michelle Hatch, hairstylist

Once you've read this book, you will be well on your way to understanding what kind of career you want, what you can expect from it, and how to go about planning and beginning your path.

Where Do You Start?

To launch your career in cosmetology, you will need at minimum a high school degree or equivalent such as a General Educational Development (GED) certification. In addition, each state requires cosmetologists (including barbers and hairstylists) to complete a program in a licensed cosmetology school. These are taught in vocational schools and community colleges and typically take two years to complete. On graduation, you will receive a certificate.

However, education in cosmetology is ongoing and career-long. Many professionals continue to take courses or seminars to keep their skills sharp and stay on top of new trends and techniques. It is definitely not a profession you want to fall behind in!

TIP: A college degree is not a requirement for a career in cosmetology, but if you are interested in pursuing a bachelor's degree and may want to start your own business, such as a nail saloon, a degree in business or marketing will be a strong asset in helping you succeed.

Choosing the right career will also depend on your personality and interests outside work such as whether you work better with people or independently; whether you want to be the boss or work for someone you admire; and what you want your life to include outside working hours—including hobbies and other activities that are important to you.

After high school, knowing how to choose and apply to vocational training such as an apprenticeship or a college program will be the next step in your path. The information in chapter 3 will help you navigate this important stage and know what questions to ask, how to best submit yourself as a candidate, and how to communicate skillfully when letting future employers or trainers understand who you are and what your potential is.

Thinking about the future and your profession is exciting and also a bit daunting. With this book, you will be on track for understanding and following the steps to get yourself on the way to a happy and successful future in the cosmetology industry. Let's get started!

1

Why Choose a Career in Cosmetology?

*I*t is never too early to start thinking about what you might like to do for a living, what kind of career path you might want to follow, and what kind of future you see for yourself. The career you choose should be one that reflects your interests, passions, natural talents, and personality so the earlier you begin to consider these, the greater a head start you will have in discovering your dream job.

The fact that you picked this book up and are reading it means you have recognized that you are interested in taking your passion for beauty, style, health, creativity, and helping people to the next level by considering cosmetology as a career. You're already off to a great start.

Choosing a career is a difficult task, but as we discuss in more detail in chapter 2, there are many methods and means of support to help you refine your career goal and hone in on a profession that will be satisfying and will fit you the best. Of course, the first step is understanding what a particular field—in this case cosmetology—actually encompasses and learning what the outlook of the profession looks like. That is the emphasis of this chapter, which looks at defining the field in general and then more specifically while also examining the past and the predicted future of the field.

"Cosmetology," as mentioned in the introduction, is a broad term for an industry that includes many different roles and specializations. Although you may automatically imagine yourself working as a hairstylist in a salon—perhaps your own salon—you may also find yourself working as a hair or makeup stylist for weddings, the theater, or film; working as a nail technician; or owning your own spa. The ways in which society creates demand for all things cosmetology are virtually endless, and that's good news for your career outlook.

It also gives you more options to sort through. What kind of cosmetology work are you interested in? What kind of work schedule do you want to have?

Do you want to work for yourself or for a corporation? Where do you see yourself living? These are all factors to consider.

As with any career, there are pros and cons to the cosmetology business, which we will discuss in this chapter. When balancing the good points and the less-attractive points of a career, you must ask yourself whether, in the end, the positives outweigh any negatives you may discover. This chapter will also help you decide whether a career in the field of cosmetology is actually the right choice for you. And if you decide it is, chapter 2 will offer suggestions on how to prepare for your career path, including questions to ask yourself and resources to help you determine more specifically what kind of career related to cosmetology will suit you the very best.

What Is Cosmetology?

The word "cosmetology" has several origins. According to the Online Etymology Dictionary,[1] the word means the "'art or practice of beauty culture,' 1855, from French *cosmétologie*, from Latinized form of Greek *kosmetos* 'well-ordered,' from *kosmein* 'to arrange, adorn,' from *kosmos* 'order; ornament.'"

In ancient Rome, female workers who were charged with beautifying their mistresses were called *cosmetae*.

The field (and study) of cosmetology refers to the creation and application of beauty treatments. This can entail hairstyling, skin care, makeup, nail care, and even hair removal.

Women and men alike have decorated themselves cosmetically since the dawn of time using various ingredients along the way, and today the beauty industry is worth more than a whopping $530 billion.[2] Here are some other impressive stats.[3]

- The cosmetics industry is growing more than ever and is expected to have a market value of almost $805 billion by 2023.
- Experts consider the beauty industry to be one of the few recession-proof industries.

IS THE BEAUTY INDUSTRY REALLY RECESSION-PROOF?

Despite the economic crisis of 2008, the beauty industry managed to grow in the years that followed. According to U.S. Census data, between 2007 and 2009 in the United States, there was a 14.4 percent increase in the number of beauty salons. Talking to CNN,[5] Tarsa Scott, a hairstylist in Maryland, said, "Most people—especially women—even when there are bad times, we want to feel good. We're not going to sacrifice feeling beautiful just because we're in a bad situation."

In 2009, U.S. News & World Report listed "hairstylist" as one of the thirty best careers,[6] giving it high scores for job satisfaction, artistic expression, and job stability, and ranking it number 23 in a listing of best jobs without a college degree.

It seems no matter what, people will make seeing their stylist a priority—it's considered by many to be a crucial aspect of self-care, especially in harder times when it's important to feel good. George Miller, an educator at the beauty school Salon Success Academy,[7] agrees: "I call being a stylist the chosen profession. Think about it. You have to go see your doctor once a year. You have to go see your dentist twice a year. But you go see your hairstylist every six weeks. I know a lot of people who can't live without seeing their stylist that often."

The demand for services in the cosmetology industry is expected to remain high in the future, which bodes well for job security. GETTY IMAGES/SKYNESHER.

- In 2019, the cosmetics industry was worth $93.5 billion in the United States—an increase of $74.7 million from 2018.
- The sale of personal-care products, or toiletries, is growing and is expected to reach $500 billion by 2020.
- According to beauty industry growth statistics, the number of employees in the service segment is expected to increase by 10 percent for barbers, hairdressers, and cosmetologists and by almost 22 percent for massage therapists by 2024.

Clearly there is a great interest in beauty treatments in the United States and elsewhere. And it's not just women who are running to salons to have a professional take care of their hair, skin, nails, and unwanted body hair: while women make up the majority of salon customers (72 percent of women versus 52 percent of men have used professional care services, according to 2012 data from Mintel[4]), a growing number of male-focused salons have been drawing a male clientele interested in similar services.

A Brief Look at Cosmetology in Ancient Times

The desire to look and feel beautiful is hardly a recent phenomenon. As far back as historians can go in time, people have found ways to improve their looks, care for their hygiene, and obtain a healthful, pleasing appearance. Here's a brief walk through the history of what we now refer to as cosmetology.

- 4000 BC: As far back as this, the Egyptians were creating makeup using natural materials such as malachite, which is a copper ore that they used to create greenish "eye shadow," and kohl, which was used to make thick, black lines to shape the eyes.
- 3000 BC: In China, people began staining their nails with various substances, including bees' wax and egg whites, and the color of your nails came to represent your social class.
- 500 BC: Ancient Greeks took their vanity seriously, using perfumes and cosmetics for virtually everything, from personal grooming to religious rites to medical purposes. They had already developed methods for caring for their hair, nails, and skin.

Historians can trace our use of beauty products and cosmetics back to 4000 BC.
GETTY IMAGES/NICOOLAY.

- 500 BC: In ancient Rome, white skin was considered a beauty standard, and women went to great lengths to achieve this. Women often applied face whiteners, some of which (like white lead) are now known to be toxic. They also used other substances, including crocodile dung and powdered chalk.

Women from Sparta, a city in Greece, were forbidden to wear makeup at all because they were considered to have a natural, flawless beauty (as well as being highly intelligent) and it was thought that additional beauty through makeup would just be unfair.

- In the eighth century AD: dye from henna plants was used to decorate the hands and feet of women in marriage ceremonies and for protection from evil. This trend spread across Africa, the Middle East, and India and continues to be popular in many regions today.[8]

The Dawn of Modern Cosmetology

The health and beauty industry is thriving around the world. There are many job titles and functions that fall under the broad term "cosmetology," and many professionals provide more than one service. Although this book will cover as many of these careers as possible, it will focus mostly on the following.

- hairstylist
- nail technician
- salon or spa manager
- beautician

- wedding and event stylist
- makeup artist
- esthetician

The Pros and Cons of the Cosmetology Field

As with any career you can choose, there are positive and less-positive aspects to a career in cosmetology. Of course, this all depends on the individual: what might be a negative for some might be a positive for others and the other way around. In this section, we will mention some of the pros and cons of a career in cosmetology, but of course you should consider them for yourself and decide whether they are actually attractive or unattractive points and, ultimately, whether the good outweighs the less good when you imagine yourself launching your career in the field.

TIP: Although it's one thing to read about the pros and cons of a particular career, the best way to really get a feel for what a typical day on the job is like and what the challenges and rewards are is to talk to someone who is already working in the profession or who has in the past.

Here are some general pros.

- You get to do what you love: be creative, learn about new trends and techniques in beauty care, and express your tastes and talents. It is a constantly evolving field with new trends and innovations and endless opportunities for learning.
- It is a highly socially interactive career. You will have the chance to spend time getting to know and chatting with your clients as you perform treatments both to make the experience more enjoyable and to get to know their likes and tastes so you can deliver the result they want.
- You will have colleagues who share your passion and from whom you can learn.
- The job-market outlook is very good.
- There's a vast variety of work environments, from corporations to self-employment.
- It's a field you can enter without having a college degree.

And here are some general cons.

- Physically, a career as a cosmetologist can be challenging. You can expect to spend a lot of time on your feet as you work with clients.
- Because beauty care is very personal, you can expect your clients to be very particular about the treatments they receive and the results they get. Be prepared to deal at times with clients who may be a little, um, difficult.
- It is an extremely competitive field, and breaking in and then advancing to the next level can take a lot of time, hard work, and patience.
- Your working week may not be a set nine to five, Monday through Friday. Be prepared to work weekends and sometimes evenings.

"Being able to be creative and inspire people and watch people grow is a beautiful thing to be lucky enough to witness. Being a hairstylist has never felt like work to me since it has always been fun. There is nothing more rewarding than seeing a client happy with how they look and watching them walk out feeling more confident and smiling."—Kendra Meyer, salon owner

How Healthy Is the Job Market for the Cosmetology Industry?

For the most part, the job-market outlook for the cosmetology industry is very healthy. For one thing, people will always want to look their best, feel beautiful, and have healthy skin, hair, and nails. Be it for special events, photo shoots, daily life, job interviews, and so on, the demand for cosmetology services is unlikely to ever lessen. This means there is plenty of room for more creative, inventive professionals in the field.

Many people consider treatments once thought luxuries, such as a manicure, necessities today. A person's appearance, beyond simple vanity, is important in determining how they present themselves, such as in a job interview, and how they feel about themselves. Because of this, personal appearance is expected to continue to be an important aspect of life and one that people will always be willing to spend money on.

The BLS[9] predicts the demand for the "personal appearance worker"—which includes all aspects of cosmetology and beauty care—will grow at least 13 percent overall between 2016 and 2026. That's a significant number and higher than that of many other industries. The BLS expects an average of 115,600 new openings in the cosmetology industry due to both growth and the job opportunities created when others leave the profession.

While all of this is good, at the same time cosmetology is a competitive field and one that requires flexibility of hours and continuous learning and training. Still, when comparing cosmetology to other careers in the United States, the BLS predicts positive growth—in some cases above the average for all careers—for the job market in the cosmetology industry. What follows are statistics published by the BLS and Payscale about specific careers in the field.

HAIRSTYLIST[10]

A hairstylist, as the name implies, is charged with styling hair, which can include cutting, styling, treating, and coloring hair. Many hairstylists choose to specialize in one of these skills, though many are also generalists.
- hourly pay: $11.94
- annual wage: $24,830
- projected job-market growth (2018–2028): 8 percent, faster than average

WHEN HAIR IS NOT JUST HAIR:
ICONIC HAIRSTYLES ACROSS TIME

Throughout time, hair has been an essential part of a person's image, expression of personality, and cultural and "tribal" identification, and an element of what makes them feel good about themselves. Some hairstyles have had a greater impact than others and have become almost synonymous with those who wore them—both real people and fictional characters. Their hairstyle came to represent a moment in time, what that person stood for, or what they were trying to achieve. Here are a few examples of such iconic, sometimes infamous, moments in hair.

- Medusa. A prime example of hair that is so bad it's empowering. This mythological character sported a head full of snakes. Her hair was both hideous and scary enough to make her one of the most feared characters in Greek mythology.
- Rapunzel. This well-known fairy-tale princess had hair so long it was her only tie to the world below her isolated tower. But it was also so beautiful it attracted a prince who, as fairy tales go, was her true love. He was able to climb up and ultimately save her using her long locks.
- Jennifer Aniston. Skipping ahead many, many years, this actress played the character of Rachel in the enormously popular and enduring sitcom *Friends* that was launched in the 1990s. Her haircut was so tied to her role that it became known worldwide as "the Rachel."
- Veronica Lake. Wearing what were known as "peekaboo bangs," this film noire star used her bangs, which hung over her eyes, to add to her mystery and seductiveness quite effectively.
- Shirley Temple. Arguably the world's most famous child-star, Shirley Temple charmed the world with her iconic, bouncy, full locks of curly hair, making this little star irresistible.
- Angela Davis. Proving that hair has political power as well as a purely aesthetic appeal, in the 1960s and 1970s in the United States, the afro became a symbol of the black power and black is beautiful movements.
- The Beatles. Because it is not only women who draw attention with their haircuts, we would be remiss in not mentioning the Fab Four and the stir caused by what was at the time considered long and rebellious hair—although by today's standards, it does not seem so shocking. At the time, it made them one of the most recognizable bands in the world.

NAIL TECHNICIAN[11]

A nail technician, also called a manicurist (fingernails) or pedicurists (toenails) is specialized in the treatment (cleaning and shaping) and beautifying of nails, such as with polish.

- annual wage: $24,330
- projected job-market growth (2018–2028): 10 percent, faster than average

BEAUTICIAN[12]

A beautician can work in a salon as a hairstylist but can also specialize in other services, including beauty and personal-care services such as brow waxes and other waxes as well as makeup application.

- hourly pay: $12.11
- annual wage: $29,000
- projected job-market growth (2018–2028): 8 percent, average

WEDDING AND EVENT STYLIST[13]

A wedding and event stylist is a professional hired specifically to do the hair and makeup for a special event, such as a wedding.

- hourly pay: $10.17
- annual wage: $38,488
- projected job-market growth (2018–2028): 8 percent, faster than average

MAKEUP ARTIST[14]

A makeup artist is skilled in applying makeup for various occasions or purposes and may work in television, the theater, or film.

- hourly pay: $18.44
- annual wage: $45,000
- projected job-market growth (2018–2028): 8 percent, faster than average

SKIN-CARE SPECIALIST[15]

A skin-care specialist focuses on the health and beautification of the skin. They are also called *estheticians.*

WHAT IS A MEDIAN INCOME?

Throughout your job search, you might hear the term "median income" used. What does it mean? Some people believe it's the same thing as average income, but that's not correct. While median income and average income might sometimes be similar, they are calculated in different ways.

Median income is the income for which half of the workers earn more than that income and the other half of workers earn less. If this seems complicated, think of it this way: Suppose there are five employees in a company, each with varying skills and experience. Here are their salaries.

- $42,500
- $48,250
- $51,600
- $63,120
- $86,325

What is the median income? In this case, the median income is $51,600 because of the five incomes listed, it is in the middle. Two salaries are higher than $51,600 and two are lower.

Average income is simply the sum of all the salaries ($291,795) divided by the total number of salaries (5). In this case, the average income is $58,359.

Why does this matter? Median income is a more accurate way to measure the various incomes in a set because it's less likely to be influenced by extremely high or low numbers in the group of salaries. For example, in our example of five incomes, the highest income ($86,325) is much higher than the other incomes and therefore it makes the average income ($58,359) higher than many of the incomes in the group as well. Therefore, if you base your income expectations on the average, you'll likely be disappointed to eventually learn that most incomes are below it.

But if you look at median income, you'll always know that half the people are above it and half are below it. That way, depending on your level of experience and training, you'll have a better estimate of where you'll end up on the salary spectrum.

Am I Right for a Cosmetology Career?

It's the million-dollar question, and the answer can really only come from you. But don't despair: there are plenty of resources both online and elsewhere that can help you find the answer by guiding you through the types of questions and considerations that will bring you to your conclusion. These are covered in more detail in chapter 2. But for now, let's look at the general demands and responsibilities of a cosmetology career and suggest some questions that may help you discover whether such a profession may be a good match for your personality, interests, and the general lifestyle you want to have in the future.

Of course, no job is going to match your personality or fit your every desire, especially when you are just starting out. There are, however, some aspects of a job that may be so unappealing or simply wrong for you that you may decide to opt for something else, or equally you may be so drawn to one feature of a job that the job's downsides are not that important.

Obviously, having an ability and a passion for hair care, nail care, skin care, and so on in any capacity is key to success in this field, but there are other factors to keep in mind. One way to see if you may be cut out for a career in cosmetology is to ask yourself the following questions.

- Am I happy standing most of the day, or would I prefer to be sitting behind a desk?
- Regardless of the type of treatment you provide as a professional cosmetologist, you can expect it to be physically demanding. Whether standing at a hairstylist station or bending down to treat someone's toenails, you will not be sitting comfortably in an ergonomic chair most of your working days.
- When something goes wrong, can I think quickly on my feet to find a solution?
- In any type of career where you are providing a service to a customer, being able to problem-solve under pressure (and not making a situation worse by letting the customer see, for example, a panicked response to a hair coloring gone wrong) will be key to your success.
- Am I a highly creative person who is also able to let an idea I may love go because others disagree or it just isn't possible?

- "The customer is always right." Although as a creative professional you will have your own vision, understand you will have to compromise with the customer to ensure you get a result that satisfies them while allowing you to showcase your skills and expertise.
- Am I willing to keep up with the required licenses and continue learning new styles and techniques?
- In the field of cosmetology, you will be expected to learn constantly. Refining techniques, keeping up with new products and styles, and of course keeping any required licenses up to date will be necessary.
- Can I consistently deal with people in a professional, friendly way?
- Communication is a key skill to have in any profession but particularly in a customer-service-oriented job.

WORK HARD, BE DEPENDABLE, BE HUNGRY FOR SUCCESS

Michelle Hatch was born and raised in Malden, Massachusetts, and attended a family-owned cosmetology school there. She was licensed in 1989 and worked in the hair industry for a few years before she fell into the corporate world in Cambridge, Massachusetts, for ten years. She moved to Cape Cod in 2001 after a divorce to start anew and knew her passion was not behind a desk. That kick-started her creative side, and she went back into the salon. She has been on Cape Cod for eighteen years, twelve of them spent behind the chair at Headlines Salon and Day Spa in Falmouth, and she has built a happy and fulfilling life for herself doing what she loves to do, which is making people feel and look their best!

Michelle Hatch. MICHELLE HATCH.

She lives a considerably active lifestyle. Being physically active and saying yes to new experiences is important to her. She is also very close to her family: her amazing parents, two sisters, brothers-in-law, and two nieces. And let's not forget her dogs and how profoundly important they are to her. She loves them so much. Hard work, perseverance, and a tough skin have allowed her some pretty amazing experiences. She enjoys traveling to Europe and plans to do even more.

Why did you choose to become a hairdresser?

Truth be told, it was never something I aspired to be growing up. I had no interest in college because I had no vision of what I was passionate about just yet. I knew I was a visual, creative person but I was too immature to realize I had a talent for artistry in some capacity. I went to cosmetology school a year after I graduated from high school simply because I had to make a move and it was trendy at the time. I was buying time, needing to figure out what I wanted to do with my life. My father was always vocal about how important the trades are. I could never have imagined how much I would love what I do.

What is a typical day on the job for you?

I think many people assume being a hairstylist is easy and we sit around gossiping all day and "cutting hair." That idea is a cliché and not accurate at all! Typically, I like to get to work a half hour before my first client to prepare for my day. Nothing worse than your clients seeing you coming in late and flustered. Fortunately, I have a substantial clientele so I'm busy all day. Appointment timing is every fifteen minutes for me so I can manage two clients at a time. Lots of hustle! Staying on track is important to keep the rest of my day rolling and not run behind. It's a lot of work and standing and sometimes trying to find small pockets in the day to eat but I don't mind. I prefer the bustle of it all.

What's the best part of your job?

When I meet a new client and she's feeling down, just had a baby, feeling drab, whatever the case may be, I sit and talk to her and really consult. I can't do much about personal situations, but if I can make someone feel and look beautiful, *that* is the best. Many times women prefer to talk to their stylist about personal things going on at home. They know we are there to listen, not to judge or analyze. There are great friendships built in a hairdresser's chair, and to give them a new look, which makes them feel good, is just the icing.

What's the worst or most challenging part of your job?

With any job there are challenges, especially when dealing with the public. For me, an argumentative client is most challenging. And there are many. Dealing with that kind of a situation is tricky. I try and maintain my professionalism and a level of calm. There are people who seem to see us as nothing more than "just a hairdresser," which is a very real part of being one. There are clients who, no matter what you do and how much you cater to them, will never be happy with your work. I used to take this personally but learned over the years that their behavior in my chair rarely has anything to do with me or my work. You have to have a tough skin in this business!

What's the most surprising thing about your job?

Surprising and flattering is when you realize the magnitude of how important you are in your client's lives. Its always such a little "Whoa!" moment! A client shared with me that I was one of her passwords on one of her accounts! Which I just found amusing. They listen and care about you as well. Significant moments in my life, my clients have supported me. Happy times, sad times, and all in between. My clients find the kindest, most thoughtful ways to let me know how they feel.

What kinds of qualities do you think one needs to be successful at this job?

Number one is personality. I can't stress that enough. Women by nature want to come in and relax and unwind, laugh a little and chat! There are many diverse personalities in my chair so I make it a point to make them feel they are my only focus. I give them undivided attention and try and stay current with news, pop culture, movies, and music. It can be awkward when there is just silence unless you can read the person and get the feeling they would rather not engage. Other than that, let your personality do the work, but keep it professional.

How do you combat burnout?

Vacations! I work forty-plus hours a week. Go go go! I love it. However, burnout is real and it happens often and too soon in this profession. I can feel when I'm getting overloaded. I take a couple of small vacations and one big one in the fall. Summertime where I work and live is pandemonium, so by the time the summer ends, my tank is empty. I like to take ten to fifteen days to recharge. It's essential to be sure you take care of yourself too!

What would you tell a young person who is thinking about becoming a hairstylist?

You have to have a strong work ethic and you must have patience. I've seen it time and time again. New stylists get out of school and assume they will be put behind a chair with a full clientele right away. Many spas and salons will start you off as an assistant. Its not very glamorous but it's the stepping-stone for every successful hairdresser. You can't give up and walk away because you don't want to do assistant work. It's how we all learned and from the best. It's a simple formula. Work hard, be dependable, be hungry for success. It will come, and when it does, you will be so grateful and proud and then it gets glamorous!

Summary

This chapter covered a lot of ground as far as looking more closely at the various types of jobs that exist within the field of cosmetology. The chapter was generally not about each job specifically, and most of the information was relevant to the field as a whole.

In this chapter, we looked far back in history to see how the cosmetology industry was born and how it has thrived. We looked at some of the unique demands of the profession and asked you to question whether you think it is for you.

Here are two ideas to take away with you as you move on to the next chapter.

- The field of cosmetology is a broad one and there are many specializations you can choose from within it.
- The BLS predicts healthy job-market growth for many roles within the industry.

Given all you now know about cosmetology-related professions, you may still be questioning whether such a career is right for you. This chapter provided some questions that can help you visualize yourself in the real-world situations you can expect to face on the job.

Assuming you are now more enthusiastic than ever about pursuing a career in cosmetology, in the next chapter, we will look more closely at how you can refine your choice to a more specific job within the industry. It offers tips and advice on how to find the role and work environment that will be most satisfying to you and identifies the steps you can start taking—immediately!—toward reaching your future career goals.

2

Forming a Career Path

Choosing a career is one of the most significant decisions you will ever make and one that will have a great impact on your future: where you live, how much you earn, what schedule you keep, the people who will become your colleagues and inspire and influence you throughout your professional working years. Although some people do alter career paths down the line, decisions you make early will still affect your future course.

It's a difficult decision to make, no question about that. If you already know you have a strong interest in a particular area, you are already on your way to refining your choices. But especially if you have many passions and interests, it can be hard to narrow your options down.

That you are reading this book means you have decided to investigate a career in the cosmetology industry, which means you have already discovered a passion for creativity, artistic flair, style, fashion, helping and interacting with people, and ongoing learning. But even within the cosmetology industry, there are many choices, including what role you want to pursue, what work environment you desire, and what type of work schedule will best fit your lifestyle.

Cosmetology encompasses many different specializations, work environments, and areas of expertise. If you decide you want to focus on skin care, you will need less knowledge of hair coloring techniques than if that were to be your specialty. You may want to work full-time in a salon each day, or you may find yourself doing hair and makeup for film, television, or the theater, which would mean doing contract work and likely traveling or working varying hours. You may want to own your own waxing salon or work as a freelance event stylist. Or perhaps you want to be a generalist, someone who knows how to provide an array of beauty services. The point is, choosing cosmetology as a career path is a big step toward knowing what you want in your future, but there are still many choices to make within that field and what your path should be in making your dream come to life.

Before you can plan your path to a successful career in the cosmetology industry, it's helpful to develop an understanding of what role you want to have and in what environment you wish to work. How much education would you like to pursue? Depending on your ultimate career goal, the steps to getting there differ. Do you want to attend a cosmetology program at a community college, or would you be better off applying to a well-established cosmetology school? Do you want to pursue a bachelor's degree (a four-year commitment) and then attend beauty school after graduation? There are a lot of options, once again.

Deciding on a career means asking yourself big questions, but there are tools and assessment tests that can help you determine what your personal strengths and aptitudes are and with which career fields and environments they best align. These tools will guide you to think about important factors in choosing a career path such as how you respond to pressure (and how effectively) and how much you enjoy working and communicating with people.

This chapter explores the educational and licensing requirements for various careers within the cosmetology industry as well as options for where to go for help when planning your path to the career you want. It offers advice on how to begin preparing for your career path at any age or stage in your education, including high school.

Planning the Plan

So where to begin? Before taking the leap and applying to college or cosmetology school, there are other considerations and steps you can take to map out your plan for pursing your career. Preparing your career plan begins with developing a clear understanding of what your actual career goal is.

Planning your career path means asking yourself questions that will help shape a clearer picture of what your long-term career goals are and what steps to take in order to achieve them. When considering these questions, it's important to prioritize your answers—when listing your skills, for example, put them in order of strongest to weakest. When considering questions relating to how you want to balance your career with the rest of your life, such as family and hobbies, really think about what your top priorities are and in what order.

HAIR REMOVAL'S LONG, CONTROVERSIAL HISTORY

Like all trends relating to beauty, from hairstyles to fake nails, the history of hair removal is a long one, dating back to ancient Roman and Greek days, and even earlier. Copper razors from as early as 3000 BC have been found in India and were used to remove body hair—including hair on the heads of women—that was considered unsightly.

Tweezers next entered the scene, becoming the favorite means of hair removal for upper-class Roman women in the sixth century. One of the first appearances of waxing as a means of removing unwanted body hair was among Egyptian women around the time of Cleopatra, who used a mixture made mostly of sugar in a way similar to modern waxing practices.

In addition to hair on the legs or underarms, women far back in history removed hair from their heads, their foreheads, and more, all to achieve what was considered an ideal, hairless beauty. In the early 1900s, this ideal of smooth, hairless skin was considered a key aspect of a woman's attractiveness and desirability. And as fashions changed and women were "permitted" to expose more of their bodies—shorter skirts, for example, in the 1920s—hair removal became that much more important.

Armpit hair was thought to be unsightly in the early 1900s. Advertisements for hair-removal products began appearing in woman's magazines, and the first razor designed especially for women came on the market.

By the 1960s, 98 percent of woman were shaving their legs, a result, no doubt, of the miniskirt craze.

Today many hair-removal options exist, including tweezing, waxing, and threading as well as the use of epilators and lasers, which can achieve permanent hair removal.

YOUR PASSIONS, ABILITIES, AND INTERESTS: IN JOB FORM!

Think about how you've done at school and how things have worked out at any temporary or part-time jobs you've had so far. What are you really good at in your opinion? And what have other people told you you're good at? What are you not very good at right now but would like to become better at? What are you not very good at now and okay with not getting better at?

Now forget about work for a minute. In fact, forget about needing to ever have a job again. You won the lottery—congratulations. Now answer these questions: What are your favorite three ways of spending your time? For each one of those ways, can you describe why you think you in particular are attracted to it? If you could get up tomorrow and do anything you wanted all day long, what would it be? These questions can be fun but can also lead you to your true passions. The next step is to find the job that sparks those passions.

The following are topics that it will be helpful to think about deeply when planning your career path.

- What are your interests outside a work context? How do you like to spend your free time? What inspires you? What kind of people do you like to surround yourself with and how do you best learn? What do you really love doing?
- Brainstorm a list of the various career choices within the cosmetology industry that you are interested in pursuing. Organize the list in order of which careers you find most appealing and then list what it is about each that attracts you. This can be anything from work environment to geographic location to the degree in which you would work with other people in a particular role.
- Research information on each job on your career choices list. You can find job descriptions, salary indications, career outlook, and educational requirements online, for example.
- Consider your personality traits. How do you respond to stress and pressure? Do you consider yourself a strong communicator? Do you work well in teams or prefer to work independently? Do you consider yourself creative? How do you respond to criticism? All of these are important to

keep in mind to ensure you choose a career path that makes you happy and in which you can thrive.

- Consider what other factors feature in your vision of your ideal life. Think about how your career will fit in with the rest of your life, including whether you want to live in a big city or small town, how much flexibility you want in your schedule, how much autonomy you want in your work, and what your ultimate career goal is.
- The cosmetology industry is a very competitive field, particularly when you are starting out in your career. Because it requires so much commitment, it's important to think about how willing you will be to put in long hours and perform what can be very demanding work. It also requires a lot of self-promotion and confidence to secure a client base that will be loyal to you.
- Although money is not everything and other factors such as job satisfaction and work-life balance are very important to consider, money is something you will have to think about. What are your salary expectations, now and in the future?

Asking yourself some key questions and thinking deeply about the answers can help you make great strides in arriving at a decision about your future career path. GETTY IMAGES/SKYNEXT.

Posing these questions to yourself and thinking about them deeply and answering them honestly will help make your career goals clearer and guide you in knowing which steps you will need to take to get there.

Other Useful Courses to Pursue

Although clearly you will want to, at minimum, take a program in cosmetology at a community college or cosmetology school, there are other courses you can take that may seem unrelated to your career goals but will in fact give you usable, applicable knowledge to help you succeed even more. The following are some suggestions.

- Business classes. To better understand how to succeed in a competitive and ever-changing market, and to understand budgets and project management, branding, staff management, business strategy, and so on, taking business courses will give you an edge. This will come in handy whether you choose a freelance career—being hired for one job at a time rather than being a full-time employee—or instead want to start your own business.
- Communication courses. Be it internal communication with your team or company or communication with customers, strong communication skills are an asset in any profession. Courses such as interpersonal communication can be particularly useful for a service-oriented career, which will demand that you interact daily with clients and colleagues.
- Basic chemistry. A lot of beauty procedures involve mixing chemicals and other ingredients, such as for hair treatments. Some general knowledge of chemistry will come in handy for sure.

Where to Go for Help

The process of deciding on and planning a career path is daunting. In many ways, the range of choices of careers available today is a wonderful thing. It allows us to refine our career goals and customize them to fit our own lives and personalities. In other ways, though, too much choice can be extremely daunting and can require a lot of soul-searching to navigate clearly.

> "Every single aspect of my job is the best part: the consultation, learning about my client, deciding on my approach to the client's hair goal, and of course the process. Their reaction to the outcome of their service. Then finally, the photo session afterward. It makes me so happy to see their face when they look at the pictures I just took of them."—Taj Maxedon, hairstylist

Answering questions about your habits, characteristics, interests, and personality can be very challenging. Identifying and prioritizing all of your ambitions, interests, and passions can be overwhelming and complicated. It's not always easy to see ourselves objectively or see a way to achieve what matters most to us. But there are many resources and approaches to help guide you in drawing conclusions about these important questions.

- Take a career assessment test to help you find what career best suits you. These are available online.
- Consult with a career or personal coach to refine your understanding of your goals and how to pursue them.
- Talk with professionals working in the job you are considering and ask them what they enjoy about their work, what they find the most challenging, and what path they followed to get there.
- Educate yourself as much as possible about the industry: which styles are most popular now and which have been popular in the past (the past often informs the future) and which techniques are changing in terms of treatments. Stay abreast of the industry no matter which role you wish to pursue. The more cutting edge you are, the more in demand you will be.
- If possible, arrange to job-shadow someone working in the field you are considering. This will enable you to experience in person what the atmosphere is like, what a typical workday entails, how coworkers interact with each other and management, and how well you can see yourself thriving in that role and work culture.
- Work on your portfolio. Don't wait until you can be paid professionally to start building a body of work: haircuts, hairstyles, makeup styling, eyebrow waxing, and so forth. Hone your skills as much as you can, and build your portfolio as you go.

"Before I became an esthetician, I really liked the results of waxing. Once I started school, I was waxing my whole body at that point because we all needed the practice. I fell in love. Waxing results last much longer than shaving and I experienced so much less skin irritation than when I would shave. I think personally loving the services you offer makes it much easier to get people on board with why they would love it too!"—Bryhannon Natale, owner of Nude Wax Company

Online Resources to Help You Plan Your Path

The Internet is an excellent source for advice and assessment tools that can help you find and figure out how to pursue your career path. Some of these tools will focus on your personality and aptitude; others will help you identify and improve your skills to prepare for your career.

In addition to the sites below, you can also use the Internet to find a career or life coach near you—many coaches offer their services online as well. Job sites such as LinkedIn are a good place to search for people working in a profession you'd like to learn more about or to explore the types of jobs available in the industry.

- At www.educations.com, you will find a career test designed to help you find the job of your dreams. Visit www.educations.com/career-test to take the test.
- The Princeton Review has created a career quiz that focuses on personal interests: www.princetonreview.com/quiz/career-quiz.
- The BLS provides information, including quizzes and videos, to help students up to grade 12 explore various career paths. Visit www.bls.gov to find these resources.

Making High School Count

Once you have discovered your passion and have a fairly strong idea what type of career you want to pursue, you naturally want to start putting your career-path plan into motion as quickly as you can. If you are a high school student, you may feel there isn't much you can do toward achieving your career goals—other than, of course, earning good grades and graduating. But there are actually many ways you can make your high school years count toward your career in cosmetology. This section will cover how you can use this period of your education and life to better prepare for your career goal and to ensure you keep your passion alive while improving your skill set.

If you dream of a career in cosmetology, it's never too early to start taking steps to make it happen. Even if you haven't started high school yet, there are ways to enhance your skills and prepare yourself for your future. GETTY IMAGES/GEMENACOM.

COURSES TO TAKE IN HIGH SCHOOL

Depending on your high school and what courses you have access to, there are many subjects that will help you prepare for a career in the cosmetology industry. It's unlikely your school will have specific courses in hair care or makeup application; however, there are other courses and subjects that are just as relevant to a cosmetology career. Some of them may seem unrelated initially, but they will all help you prepare yourself and develop key skills.

- Art classes. Even though giving a person highlights or applying hair tracks for a weave is not the same as using a pencil or a paintbrush, encouraging your artistic flair in any sense will help you free your creativity in your work. Experimenting with different lines and colors can be very inspiring.
- Business and economics classes. As with any type of business, if you have the ambition to run your own, knowledge gained in business and economics classes will help you make smarter business and financial decisions.
- Interpersonal communication and public-speaking classes. These courses will be an asset to you in any profession, including the cosmetology industry. You will find yourself consulting with clients about options, selling products to customers (this is a major source of revenue for a salon), as well as interacting conversationally with customers and colleagues as you work. As cosmetology services are quite personal and your clients will *always* care about the outcome, being able to read verbal and physical communication will help you interpret how happy or comfortable your clients are as you work.
- Science classes. Understanding chemical reactions to coloring agents will be a part of your life as a colorist—especially when correcting mistakes, such as those caused by clients attempting to color or treat their own hair at home. Chemistry also plays a part in skin-care treatments and even makeup.
- Mathematics classes. Aside from using accounting and arithmetic to balance your budget if you run your own business, a knowledge of geometry might come in handy too. As a cosmetologist, you will use the principles of geometry and proportion when cutting hair, applying makeup, and shaping eyebrows, for example.

Gaining Work Experience

The best way to learn anything is to do it. When it comes to preparing for a career in the cosmetology industry, there are several options for gaining real-world experience and getting a feel for whether you are choosing the right career for you.

The one big benefit of jobs in the cosmetology industry is you don't have to land a work-experience opportunity at an established or up-and-coming salon to prove what you've got and what you can do. Rather than wait for someone to hire you to work for them, you are wise to keep working on your own, to show not only your talent but your passion. You can experiment on yourself or on a willing friend, for example, to practice your hairstyling and makeup skills.

You might also find a job in a salon before you earn your qualifications, such as by working as a receptionist, to get a sense of how the business is run and what a typical day entails.

Any experience you can find along your path will be a strong asset. Remember, this is a competitive field you want to enter into, and every advantage counts.

Tips for Creating an Online Portfolio

There are many online tools available—free and by subscription—that will help you create a photo portfolio of your work. Your portfolio is an important part of your application if you're applying to school or for a job or as a way to market yourself if you are self-employed. A strong portfolio allows you not only to showcase your work but to express who you are and how passionate you are about what you do. Your resume is important, but your portfolio is where you can really show your talent and your personal style.

Here are some tips for creating a winning portfolio that will represent your own talent and experience.

- Consider a free site-building tool such as WordPress or Wix rather than paying out money to start. These tools are sophisticated enough to help you create an eye-catching portfolio.

- Get feedback from others—clients, colleagues, fellow students, friends, professionals in the field—and consider their reactions to and advice about the effectiveness, usability, and general impression of your site.
- Don't distract from your work. Make your presentation about the images, not the interface. There are a lot of fancy features you can add to your site, but too many bells and whistles will just annoy your viewer or at minimum take the focus off your work.
- The fewer clicks it takes before your gallery is presented, the better. Let your visitor see what you've got without having to navigate or click too many times.
- Make sure your images are relevant to any job you are applying for or service you are offering and don't be afraid to shuffle them to fit.
- Make it easy to find you. Your contact info should be easily accessible from any point on your web page. You should also add links to where else you can be found, such as on Instagram or Twitter.
- Never stop creating. Revamp your site design every so often. Try to post something new as often as you can. You don't want it to look out-dated—the fresher you keep it, the more return traffic you will have.
- Don't include anything but your very best work. Better ten images that rock than a wide variety of samples that make your work quality look variable.
- Take your time with the About Me section. This is where you can let your personality and inspiration shine through. Be creative when sharing your experience and background and what generally drives you as a cosmetologist.
- Make your home page a stunner. Your home page is the first impression visitors to your portfolio will get, so make it impressive. Choose an image that represents your aesthetic and artistic personality. Let it give visitors a solid idea of the type of work you can do.

It's also a good idea to arrange to job-shadow with a professional in the field, in whichever capacity you find most interesting. This means accompanying someone to work, observing the tasks they perform, their work culture, the environment, the hours, and the intensity of the work. Talk with people you know who work in the business and learn what they love the most or find most challenging about their job. There's no better expert than someone already working professionally in your chosen field.

Educational Requirements

The type of educational path you choose to follow will depend on your specific goals. The good news about pursuing a career in cosmetology is that once you have earned a high school degree or its equivalent (such as a General Educational Development, or general education diploma, better known as a GED), you are only two years away from being qualified to work professionally. In that time, you will be required to complete a state-approved cosmetology training program and pass a state licensing exam. You can look into cosmetology schools or apply to a community college to meet the first requirement.

However, you may be dreaming of starting your own business, running a franchise, or furthering your general education before applying to a cosmetology program, and for these goals you may consider earning a bachelor's degree, which is a four-year commitment. While there are no bachelor's degree programs in cosmetology, there are other degrees that would be of use, including degrees in psychology, business, mass communication, and health-related subjects.

The Difference Between Owning Your Business and Buying a Franchise

In the cosmetology field and many others, it is possible to launch your very own business from the ground up or to opt to buy a franchise. According to www.businesslawfreeadvice.com, a franchise business is one "in which the owners, or 'franchisors,' sell the rights to their business logo, name, and model to third party retail outlets, owned by independent, third party operators, called 'franchisees.' Franchises are an extremely common way of doing business."[1]

Basically, you are buying a full package of what is a proven business (or it wouldn't become a franchise): the business name, brand, and trademark; ongoing support from the franchisor, including infrastructural, manpower, technical, and nontechnical support; and generally guidance in running the business successfully. For this, you pay a fee called "royalties" to the franchisor.

In many ways, this is an appealing proposition. It is generally cheaper than starting your own business from scratch, and it gives you a winning model with which to work as well as name recognition for your business even though how it is run will in the end be your full responsibility.

The downside to a franchise versus owning your own business is that you lose some control. You are obligated to follow certain rules set by the franchisor and to sell or use certain products. You also have to share your profits rather than keeping them all for yourself.

Franchises in the cosmetology business include Toni&Guy, Cristophe Salon, Frenchies Modern Nail Care, and Waxing the City, but there are many others.

Later in this chapter, we will discuss considerations to keep in mind when deciding what level of education is best for you to pursue. In chapter 3, we will outline in more detail the types of programs offered and the best schools to consider should you want to pursue post–high school training and certification or an associate's or a bachelor's degree.

> "My education didn't prepare me to be an entrepreneur; I think this is something more inside. Something you really have to want to do. I was the best employee you can ask for; always had lots of drive and was target-driven and passionate about making a success for my bosses, until I realized this can be mine. Hairdressing school is important to teach you basics and routine, but some of my most successful peers don't have a college diploma and do some amazing things."
> —Adam Tullett, salon owner with Toni&Guy

Why Choose a Cosmetology School?

Graduating from cosmetology or beauty school (there is no difference) and getting your state license to practice fulfills the educational requirements to begin your career as a cosmetologist.

These schools are private institutions that focus entirely on cosmetology-related topics. Because of this, it is possible to complete a program in as little as eight months, although schools vary. You can also choose to study part-time, which enables you to work as you complete the program, which can take up to two years. The benefit is, of course, each school's emphasis on cosmetology (versus programs taught at community colleges).

Keep in mind that not all cosmetology schools are alike, however. You will want to be sure any school you apply to is accredited, which means the U.S. Department of Education has approved that school's quality and integrity in teaching cosmetology. Also be sure you look into possible financial-aid opportunities, which we will cover in chapter 4.

Why Choose an Associate's Degree?

With a two-year degree—called an associate's degree—you are qualified to work in the cosmetology field once you have passed the required state licensing test. Check your local community college or search online for one that offers a cosmetology program. Attending a community college may also make it easier to receive financial aid compared with cosmetology schools, and any credits you earn may carry over to a bachelor's degree program should you choose to pursue a four-year degree.

While it's possible to complete a cosmetology training program by studying part-time for additional flexibility (allowing you to work while you study, for example), because completing this type of program—either at a community college or via a cosmetology school—demands a lot of observation, interaction, and in-person practice, the programs are generally not offered online.

Degree programs will give you a knowledge base to begin your career with and are equivalent to completing a program at a cosmetology school. One difference is that trade schools, such as cosmetology schools, focus on the coursework required for a career in cosmetology, while at a community college, you will be required to take general education courses, such as math or writing. For that reason, an associate's degree earned at a community college can take longer to earn than it will take to complete a cosmetology school program.

Why Choose a Bachelor's Degree?

A bachelor's degree, which usually takes four years to earn, is not a requirement for a career in the cosmetology industry (in fact, such degrees in cosmetology specifically do not exist). In general, though, the higher the education level you pursue, the better your odds are of advancing in your career, which means more opportunity and, often, more compensation.

The difference between an associate's and a bachelor's degree is of course the amount of time each takes to complete. To earn a bachelor's degree, a candidate must complete forty college credits compared to twenty for an associate's degree. This translates to more courses completed and a deeper exploration of degree content even though similar content is covered in both. And even with a bachelor's degree, you will still be required to complete a program in cosmetology (at a cosmetology school or community college) to earn your state license to practice.

> Even when not required, a bachelor's degree can help advance your career, giving you an edge over the competition in the field and earning you a higher starting salary than holders of an associate's degree.

HOW MUCH YOU PUT INTO YOUR JOB IS HOW MUCH YOU'LL GET BACK

Kendra Meyer. KENDRA MEYER.

Kendra Meyer is the owner of Shear by Kendra salon. Originally from Chesterton, Indiana, Kendra graduated from high school and cosmetology school in 1990. She moved to Indianapolis in 1996 and was named one of the top stylists in *Indianapolis Monthly* in 2007 and has made multiple appearances on a local television station. She has been happily married to her husband, John, for eighteen years and has two children, Sydney, fifteen, and Max, eleven. With over twenty-five years of experience working in a variety of salons and now owning her own, Kendra's love of her profession continues to grow.

Why did you choose to become a hairstylist?

Being a hairstylist was something I have known that I wanted to do since I was a little girl. I never had a desire to do anything else. I went from playing with my dolls' hair when I was very young to later doing my friends' hair for them.

I chose to be a hairstylist because I have always enjoyed being creative, and being a hair stylist is a good way to express my creativity. Every client comes in with a blank canvas and I get the opportunity to create something beautiful with it.

What is a typical day on the job for you?

I am very fortunate because of how flexible my schedule is. I always have fresh flowers, chocolate, and refreshments for my clients to make sure they are as comfortable as possible. It feels like I am spending time and talking with friends while being creative all day long. Now that I have children, I am lucky enough to have a flexible schedule, typically working three to four days a week and eight to nine hours a day.

What's the best part of your job?

The people that I meet, the stories that I hear, and the bonds that I make are what I love most. Being able to be creative and inspire people and watch people grow is a beautiful thing to be lucky enough to witness. It's the connections that I have with my clients. Being a hairstylist has never felt like work to me since it has always been fun. There is nothing more rewarding than seeing a client happy with how they look and watching them walk out feeling more confident and smiling.

What's the worst or most challenging part of your job?

The worst part is disappointing people. There are times when you get a client that is unhappy with how their style or color turned out. One of the most important aspects of this job is communication. Having to turn people down because you can't fit them into your schedule is always very difficult. Lastly, it can be saddening when a client that you have grown close to wants to try a new stylist or moves away.

What's the most surprising thing about your job?

I am often surprised by my clients' generosity: how open they can be and the connections that I am able to form. I have built so many close relationships throughout the years that they really become like a family.

What kinds of qualities do you think one needs to be successful at this job?

You need to be a people person with strong interpersonal and customer service skills. You need to have confidence and to know what it means to act professionally. Always let the clients know that you respect their time and in return know that they respect yours. Communication is the most important part of the job because what may be a half inch to you might not be so to your client.

How do you combat burnout?

You must continue to educate yourself and remember that there is always something new to learn. There are new styles, new techniques, and an endless supply of new products. Staying on top of these areas will keep you feeling refreshed and energized as well as invigorate your work.

What would you tell a young person who is thinking about becoming a hairstylist?

When you start off it's going to be very hard—it takes a long time to build a strong clientele. You can't make everyone happy, and you have to learn to be patient and caring for your client's requests. You must take advantage of on-going educational opportunities as much as you can because things are always changing and there is always more to learn. It is one of the things I love most about the job: it never gets boring. Being a hairstylist comes with so many rewards, and how much you put into it is how much you are going to get back.

Summary

This chapter covered a lot of ground in terms of how to break down the challenge of not only discovering what career within the cosmetology industry is right for you, and in what environment, capacity, and work culture you want to work, but also how best to prepare yourself for achieving your career goal.

The chapter pointed to many tools and methods that can help you navigate the confusing path to choosing a career that is right for you. It also addressed some of the specific training and educational options and requirements and expectations that will put you, no matter what your current education level or age, at a strong advantage in a competitive field.

Use this chapter as a guideline for how to best discover what type of career will be the right fit for you and to learn what steps you can already be taking to get there. Here are some tips to leave you with.

- Take time to carefully consider what kind of work environment you see yourself working in and what kind of schedule, interaction with colleagues, work culture, and responsibilities you want to have.
- There are skills that apply to all careers within the cosmetology industry such as communication skills and business know-how, as well as science. Taking courses in or getting familiar with these as soon as possible—even before high school is not too soon!—will help you in your career or educational goals.
- Learn as much as you can about the different types of jobs available in the cosmetology field. Job-shadow a professional to get a feeling for what hours they keep, what challenges they face, and what their overall job entails. Find out what education or training they completed before launching their career.
- Investigate various colleges, vocational schools, and certification options so you can better prepare yourself for the next step in your career path.
- Don't feel you have to wait until you graduate from high school to begin taking steps to accomplish your career goals. You can already begin by working on your portfolio so you can showcase your work, for example.
- Keep your work-life balance in mind. The career you choose will be one of many adult decisions you make, and ensuring that you keep all of your priorities—family, location, work schedule—in mind will help you choose the right career for you, which will make you a happier person.

In chapter 3, we go into detail about the next steps: writing a resume and cover letter, interviewing well, follow-up communications, and more. This is information you can use to secure internships, placement in college programs or cosmetology schools, summer jobs, and more. It's not just for college grads. In fact, the sooner you can hone these skills, the better off you'll be in the professional world.

Pursuing the Educational Path

*C*hoosing a career can be daunting, yes, but even once you've refined that choice, you have to make a different and equally important one: deciding on your academic path. It is a decision that not only demands understanding what kind of education or training is required for the career you want but also what kind of school or college you want to attend. There is a lot to consider as you plan your path to entering the cosmetology field.

Now that you've gotten an overview of the different degree and program options that can prepare you for your future career, this chapter will dig more deeply into how to best choose the right type of study for you. Even if you are years away from earning your high school diploma or equivalent, it's never too soon to start weighing your options, thinking about the application process, and of course taking time to really consider what kind of educational track and environment will suit you best.

According to the National Center for Education Statistics, six years after entering college for an undergraduate degree, only 60 percent of students have graduated. Barely half of those students will graduate from college in their lifetime.

By the same token, it's never been more important to get your degree. College graduates with a bachelor's degree typically earn 66 percent more than those with only a high school diploma and are also far less likely to face unemployment. Also, over the course of a lifetime, the average worker with a bachelor's degree will earn approximately $1 million more than a worker without a postsecondary education.

As mentioned in chapter 2, once you have completed high school, you will at minimum have to complete a program with a cosmetology school or community college plus obtain a state license. You can also choose to pursue a four-year bachelor's degree in any subject (there are none available in cosmetology) and then complete a cosmetology program after you earn (or while you are earning, if you can balance the two) your degree.

This chapter will give you advice on the school application process, how to prepare for any entrance exams such as the SAT or ACT that you may need to take (this applies only to bachelor's programs, not to cosmetology school or some community colleges), and how to communicate your passion, ambition, and personal experience in a personal statement, which you will need for your application to any educational institution. When you've completed this chapter, you should have a good sense of what kind of post–high school education will be right for you and how to ensure you have the best chance of being accepted at the institution of your choice.

> "The best part of my job is, by far, the confidence that radiates from my clients when their services are done. Even if they waxed an area no one sees, they hold their head higher and have that mentality of *I can do anything!* I love being a part of that."—Bryhannon Natale, esthetician

Finding a Program or School That Fits Your Personality

Before we get into the details of good schools, it's a good idea for you to take some time to consider what type of school will be best for you. Just as with your future work environment, understanding how you best learn, what type of atmosphere best fits your personality, and how and where you are most likely to succeed will play a major part in how happy you will be with your choice. This section will provide some thinking points to help you refine what kind of school or program will be the best fit for you.

The following questions apply to whatever type of post–high school training or education you wish to pursue. Answering questions like these can help you narrow your search and focus on a smaller sample of school choices. Write your answers to these questions down somewhere where you can refer to them often, such as in a notes app on your phone.

- Size: Does the size of the school matter to you? Cosmetology schools and community colleges vary in the size of their student population. Perhaps you want a bigger school that may provide more course options or a smaller school that will offer smaller classes to give you more attention from your instructor. If you are considering a bachelor's degree, know that colleges and universities range from 500 students or fewer to over 50,000 students. If you are considering a college or university, think about what size of class you would like and what the right instructor-to-student ratio will be for you.
- Community location: Would you prefer to be in a rural area, a small town, a suburban area, or a large city? How important is the location of the school in the larger world to you? Is the flexibility of an online degree attractive to you, or do you prefer more on-site, hands-on instruction?
- Length of study: How many months or years do you want to put into your education before you start working professionally?
- Housing options: If applicable, what kind of housing would you prefer? Dorms, off-campus apartments, and private homes are all common options.
- Student body: How would you want the student body to "look"? Think about coed versus all-male or all-female settings as well as the number of minorities, how many students are part-time versus full-time, and the percentage of commuter students.
- Financial aid availability and cost: Does the school provide ample opportunities for scholarships and the like? Will cost play a role in your options?
- Support services: Investigate the strength of the academic and career placement counseling services of the school.
- Special programs: Does the school offer programs for veterans or students with disabilities or special needs?

Not all of these questions are going to be important to you, and that's fine. Be sure to make a note of aspects that don't matter so much to you too, such as size or location. You might change your mind when you go to visit a school, but it's important to take note of what you're feeling to begin with.

U.S. News & World Report[1] puts it best when they say the college that fits you best is one that will do all these things.

- offer a degree that matches your interests and needs
- provide a style of instruction that matches the way you like to learn
- provide a level of academic rigor to match your aptitude and preparation
- offer a community that feels like home to you
- value you for what you do well

According to the U.S. Department of Education, as many as 32 percent of college students change colleges during the course of their educational career. This is to say that the decision you initially make is not set in stone. Do your best to make a good choice, but remember that you can change your mind, your major, and even your campus. Many students do it and go on to have great experiences and earn great degrees.

MAKE THE MOST OF SCHOOL VISITS

If it's at all practical and feasible, you should visit the schools you're considering. To get a real feel for any college or school, you need to walk around the campus or premises, spend some time in the common areas where students hang out, and if possible sit in on a few classes. You can also sign up for school tours, if available, which are typically given by current students. This is another good way to see the campus and ask questions of someone who knows. Be sure to visit the specific school or building that covers your possible major as well. The website and brochures won't be able to convey that intangible feeling you'll get from a visit.

In addition to the questions listed above, consider these questions as well, remembering to make a list of other questions that are important to you before you visit.

- Is the campus diverse?
- What is the meal plan like? What are the food options?
- Where do most of the students hang out between classes? (Be sure to visit this area.)

In order to be ready for your visit and make the most of it, consider these tips and words of advice.

- Be sure to do some research. At the least, spend some time on the school website. Make sure your questions aren't addressed adequately there first.
- Make a list of unanswered questions.
- Arrange to meet with a professor or instructor in your area of interest.
- Be prepared to answer questions about yourself and why you are interested in the school.
- Dress in neat, clean, and casual clothes. Avoid overly wrinkled clothing or anything with stains.
- Listen and take notes.
- Don't interrupt.
- Be positive and energetic.
- Make eye contact when someone speaks directly to you.
- Ask questions.
- Thank people for their time.

Finally, be sure to send thank-you notes or emails after the visit is over. Remind the recipient of your visit and thank them for their time.

Hopefully, this section has impressed upon you the importance of finding the right fit with your chosen learning institution. Take some time to paint a mental picture about the kind of school setting that will best complement your needs, then read on for specifics about each degree.

When it comes to choosing a school, accreditation matters and is something you should consider. Accreditation is basically a seal of approval to let prospective students feel sure an institution will provide a quality education that is worth their investment and will help them reach their career goals. Future employers will want to see that the program you completed has such a seal of quality so it's something to keep in mind when choosing a school.

Determining Your Educational Plan

There are many options when it comes to pursing an education in the cosmetology field. These include cosmetology schools, two-year community colleges, and four-year colleges (in an area other than cosmetology but one that will still enrich and help you in your future). This section will help you select the track that is best suited to you. Whatever you choose, you will find there are differences in cost, in the length of the program, and in what subjects you will be offered.

It's a good idea to select roughly five schools in a realistic location (for you) that offer the degree or program you want to earn or complete. If you are considering online bachelor's programs, include these programs in your list.

Be sure you research the basic GPA and SAT or ACT requirements of each school as well. Although some community colleges do not require standardized tests for the application process, others do.

If you are planning to apply to a college or program that requires the ACT or SAT, advisors recommend that students take both the ACT and the SAT test during their junior year of high school (spring at the latest). You can retake these tests and use your highest score so be sure to leave time to retake early in your senior year if needed. You want your best score to be available to all the schools you're applying to by January of your senior year, which will also enable them to consider you for any available scholarships. Keep in mind these are general timelines—be sure to check the exact deadlines and calendars of the schools to which you're applying!

Once you have found schools in a realistic location for you that offer the degree or program in question, spend some time on their website studying the requirements for admission. Important factors weighing on your decision of which schools to apply to should include whether or not you meet the requirements, your chances of getting in (but shoot high!), tuition costs and availability of scholarships and grants, location, and the school's reputation and licensure or graduation rates.

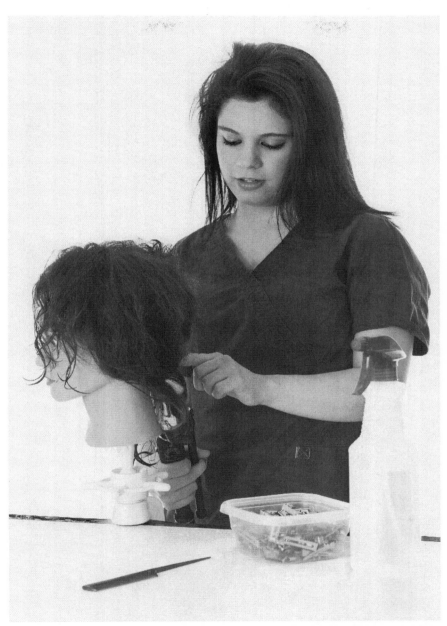

When considering which schools or programs to apply to, think about the style of learning offered by each, the size of the student body compared to the number of instructors, and other factors such as cost and location. GETTY IMAGES/MCININCH.

Many schools and colleges will list the average stats for the last class accepted to the program, which will give you a sense of your chances of acceptance.

The order of these characteristics will depend on your grades and test scores, your financial resources, work experience, and other personal factors. Taking everything into account, you should be able to narrow your list down to the institutes or schools that best match your educational or professional goals as well as your resources and other desirable factors such as location and duration of study.

Schools to Consider When Pursuing a Career in Cosmetology

Some schools and programs have a stronger reputation than others. Although you can certainly have a successful and satisfying career and experience without going to the "number one" school in your field of study, it is a good idea to shop around, to compare different schools, and to get a sense of what they offer and what features of each are the most important—to you at least.

Keep in mind that what is great for one person may not be as great for someone else. What might be a perfect school for you might be too difficult, too expensive, or not rigorous enough for someone else. Keep in mind the advice of the previous sections when deciding what you really need in a school.

While you may be interested in pursuing a bachelor's degree for whatever reason—maybe as a personal ambition to have a broader education outside cosmetology, perhaps to study business or communications to help with your cosmetology business, or perhaps to keep your options open in case you decide to change careers later—this book is specifically about cosmetology careers so we will focus on what the training and educational requirements are to achieve that goal. And even if you are planning to earn a bachelor's degree, you will still be required to complete a cosmetology program to enter the field so this information is relevant to you as well.

GREAT COSMETOLOGY SCHOOLS TO LAUNCH YOUR COSMETOLOGY CAREER

There are just under two thousand cosmetology schools in the United States. Here we'll note the names of five of the most popular beauty schools in America.

> While it is not possible to earn an associate's degree in cosmetology or complete a cosmetology school program online, some schools offer a cosmetology business associate's degree online for people who already hold a cosmetologist's license. This degree focuses more on the knowledge needed to run a successful business.

If a school you are interested in is not on one of these two lists, remember to consider the following before deciding to apply or attend.

- Will you be taking night classes or attending full-time?
- Will you be able to practice on real clients instead of just wigs?
- What is the full cost of the program?
- Is the school accredited so it can offer financial aid?
- Does the school have a continuing education program?
- Will they help you with job placement after graduation?

Here are five of the most popular and well-known beauty schools in the United States, not listed in any particular order.

- Aveda Institute
- Paul Mitchell Schools
- Empire Beauty School
- Sassoon Academy
- Ogle School

> Before choosing a school, check whether the school you are considering is included on your state's list of approved cosmetology schools—the schools that meet your state's licensing requirements. Cosmetology has 245 approved cosmetology programs! Most state boards require you complete a cosmetology program of about 1,500 hours, but keep in mind this will vary from state to state. (To become a cosmetologist in Florida, for example, you must complete a program of at least 1,200 hours versus 1,600 hours in Arizona.)

Great Associate Degree Programs to Launch Your Cosmetology Career

The curriculum for an associate's degree in cosmetology—which will usually take two years to complete—includes instruction in beauty services as well as information on identifying hair and skin disorders, sanitation, and business skills. Business classes are valuable for cosmetology students because, according to the BLS, many cosmetologists are self-employed. Some even go on to start their own personal-care businesses. Typical cosmetology classes include

- hair cutting and styling
- nail and skin care
- makeup application
- state regulations
- salon management
- health and safety

It is estimated that there are more than 1,200 community colleges in the United States,[2] and degree programs are added every year. Be sure and check your local community college (or one within a commutable distance) to see if it offers a cosmetology program.

Here is a list of five community colleges in the United States that offer associate's degree programs, not listed in any particular order. You can look up other options at https://study.com/cosmetology_schools.html.

- Sandhill Community College, Pinehurst, North Carolina
- Houston Community College Systems, Houston, Texas
- The Community College of Cosmetology, Topeka, Kansas
- San Diego City College, San Diego, California
- Pitt Community College, Winterville, North Carolina

ALL ABOUT THE COMMON APPLICATION FORM

The Common Application form is a single, detailed application form that is accepted by more than nine hundred colleges and universities in the United States. Instead of filling out a different application form for every school you want to apply to, you fill out one form and have it sent to all the schools you're interested in. The Common App itself is free, and most schools don't charge for submitting it.

If you don't want to use the Common App for some reason, most colleges will also let you apply using a form on their website. There are a few institutions that want you to apply only through their site, while other highly regarded institutions only accept the Common App. Be sure you know what the schools you're interested in want.

The Common App's website (www.commonapp.org) has a lot of useful information, including tips for first-time applicants and transfer students.

What's It Going to Cost You?

So the bottom line is what will your education end up costing you? Of course, that depends on many factors, including the type and length of degree or certification, where you attend (in-state or not, private or public institution), how much in scholarships or financial aid you're able to obtain, your family or personal income, and many other factors.

School can be an expensive investment, but there are many ways to get help paying for your education.
GETTY IMAGES/DESIGNER491.

Because the cosmetology profession is so customer-service orientated, the hiring process in some organizations will be focused, of course, on an applicant's skills, trainability, and reliability, but personality and other characteristics will come into play more than in some other professions. Some employers interviewing candidates for jobs such as hairstylist, hairdresser, barber, or cosmetologist have applicants take the Criteria Basic Skills Test (CBST) or the Customer Service Aptitude Profile (CSAP). The CBST is focused on basic job readiness and trainability skills, and the CSAP is a personality test that assesses how well a candidate's personality traits are suited to a job requiring a high level of customer interaction.

WRITING A GREAT PERSONAL STATEMENT FOR ADMISSION

The personal statement you include with your application to any college is extremely important. Write something that is thoughtful and conveys your understanding of the profession you are interested in as well as your desire to practice in this field. Why are you uniquely qualified? Why are you a good fit for this school? This essay should be highly personal (it's a "personal" statement after all). Will the admissions professionals who read it, along with hundreds of other statements, come away with a snapshot of who you really are and what you are passionate about?

Look online for examples of good ones. This will give you a feel for what works. Be sure to check your specific school for length guidelines, format requirements, and any other guidelines they expect you to follow.

And of course, be sure to proofread it several times then ask a professional (such as an instructor at your school writing center or your local librarian) to proofread it as well.

Financial Aid: Finding Money for Education

Finding the money to attend college, whether it is a two- or four-year program or a vocational career college (such as cosmetology school), can seem overwhelming. But you can do it if you have a plan before you actually start applying to college. If you get into your top-choice school, don't let the sticker cost turn you away. Financial aid can come from many different sources and it's available to cover all the different kinds of costs you'll encounter during your years in college, including tuition, fees, books, and other necessities.

The good news is that schools often offer incentive or tuition-discount aid to encourage students to attend. The market is often competitive in the favor of the student, and schools respond by offering more generous aid packages to a wider range of students than they used to. Here are some basic tips and pointers on the financial-aid process.

- You apply for financial aid during your senior year. You must fill out the Free Application for Federal Student Aid (FAFSA),[3] which can be filed starting October 1 of your senior year until June of the year you graduate. Because the amount of available aid is limited, it's best to apply as soon as you possibly can. See www.fafsa.gov to get started.
- Be sure to compare the offers you get from different schools. Your first offer for aid may not be the best you'll get.
- Wait until you receive all offers from your top schools and then use this information to negotiate with your top choice to see if they will match or beat the best aid package you received.
- To be eligible to keep and maintain your financial-aid package, you must meet certain grade or GPA requirements. Be sure you are very clear on these academic expectations and keep up with them.
- You must reapply for federal aid every year.

Watch out for scholarship scams! You should never pay to submit the FAFSA ("Free" is in its name) or be required to pay a lot to find appropriate aid and scholarships. These should be free services. If an organization promises you you'll get aid or that you have to "act now or miss out," these are both warning signs of a less reputable organization.

Also, be careful with your personal information to avoid identity theft as well. Simple things like closing and exiting your browser after visiting sites where you have entered personal information (like www.fafsa.gov) goes a long way, especially on a public computer. Don't share your student-aid ID number with anyone either.

NOT ALL FINANCIAL AID IS CREATED EQUAL

Educational institutions tend to define financial aid as any scholarship, grant, loan, or paid employment that helps students pay their college expenses. Notice that "financial aid" covers both *money you have to pay back* and *money you don't have to pay back*. That's a big difference!

Do Not Have to Be Repaid
- scholarships
- grants
- work-study

Have to Be Repaid with Interest
- federal government loans
- private loans
- institutional loans

It's important to understand the different forms of financial aid that are available to you. That way you'll know how to apply for different kinds and get the best financial-aid package that fits your needs and strengths. The two main categories that financial aid falls under are *gift aid*, which doesn't have to be repaid, and *self-help aid*, which is either loans that must be repaid or work-study funds that are earned. The next sections cover the various types of financial aid that fit in one of these areas.

Some of these forms of financial aid will not apply to community colleges or cosmetology schools. It's important to investigate the financial-support options that are available for the school and study of your choice.

GRANTS

Grants typically are awarded to students who have financial needs but they can also be used in the areas of athletics, academics, demographics, veteran support, and special talents. They do not have to be paid back. Grants can come from federal agencies, state agencies, specific universities, and private organizations. Most federal and state grants are based on financial need.

Examples of grants are the Pell Grant, SMART Grant, and the Federal Supplemental Educational Opportunity Grant (FSEOG). Visit the U.S. Department of Education Federal Student Aid site (https://studentaid.ed.gov/types/grants-scholarships) for lots of current information on grants.

SCHOLARSHIPS

Scholarships are merit-based aid that does not have to be paid back. They are typically awarded for academic excellence or some other special talent, such as in music or art. Scholarships can also be athletic-based, minority-based, awarded as aid for women, and so forth. These are typically not awarded by federal or state governments but instead come from the specific school you are applying to as well as private and nonprofit organizations.

Be sure to reach out directly to the financial-aid officers of the schools you want to attend. These people are great contacts who can lead you to many more sources of scholarships and financial aid. Visit www.gocollege.com/financial-aid/scholarships/types/ for lots more information on how scholarships in general work.

LOANS

Many types of loans are available—especially to students who need to pay for their post-secondary education. However, the important thing to remember here is that loans must be paid back with interest. Be sure you understand the interest rate you will be charged. This is the extra cost of borrowing the money and is usually a percentage of the amount you borrow. Is the interest fixed or will it change over time? Are the loan and interest deferred until you graduate (meaning you don't have to begin paying the loan off until after you graduate)? Is the loan subsidized (meaning the federal government pays the interest until you graduate)? These are all points you need to be clear on before you sign on the dotted line.

There are many types of loans offered to students, including need-based loans, non-need-based loans, state loans, and private loans. Two very reputable federal loans are the Perkins Loan and the Direct Stafford Loan. For more information on student loans, start at https://bigfuture.collegeboard.org/pay-for-college/loans/types-of-college-loans.

FINANCIAL-AID TIPS

- Some colleges and universities offer tuition discounts to encourage students to attend—so tuition costs can be lower than they look at first.
- Apply for financial aid during your senior year of high school. The sooner you apply, the better your chances.
- Compare offers from different schools—one school may be able to match or improve on another school's financial-aid offer.
- Keep your grades up—a good GPA helps a lot when it comes to merit scholarships and grants.
- You have to reapply for financial aid every year, so you'll be filling out that FAFSA form again!
- Look for ways that loans might be deferred or forgiven—service commitment programs are a way to use service to pay back loans.

FEDERAL WORK-STUDY

The U.S. Federal Work-Study Program provides part-time jobs to undergraduate and graduate students with financial need so they can earn money to pay for educational expenses. The focus of such work is on community service work and work related to a student's course of study. Not all colleges and universities participate in this program, so be sure to check with the school financial-aid office if this is something you are counting on. The sooner you apply, the more likely you are to get the job you desire and be able to benefit from the program, as funds are limited. See https://studentaid.ed.gov/sa/types/work-study for more information on this opportunity.

HELPING OTHERS SEE HOW AMAZING THEY ARE

Taj Maxedon, originally from Palo Alto, California, spent twenty-five years in the medical field before deciding in her mid-forties to attend school to become a hairstylist in Arizona. She has been working as a stylist now for seven years. She is well known for her holistic approach to hair artistry, holding a current license and practicing in Florida, Arizona, and California. She specializes in color and authenticating her clients' visual story. She wants her clients' "everyday people" to see them a little differently.

Taj Maxedon. TAJ MAXEDON.

Why did you choose to become a hairstylist?

I wanted the opportunity to help people feel better about themselves and give the right impression. I love to encourage people, bringing out the best in them. It brings me so much joy to help others see themselves as the amazing people I see in them. This is my craft, I've spend many years honing it; but I love it so much, it often doesn't feel like "work."

What is a typical day on the job for you?

An early wake up, coffee already brewing. A brisk four- to five-mile walk. Shower, feed the dogs, and I'm out the door heading to the salon for for to five highlights or a couple of color corrections that day.

What's the best part of your job?

Every single aspect. The consultation, learning about my client. Deciding on my approach to our hair goal and of course the process. Their reaction to the outcome of their service. Then finally, the photo session afterward. It makes me so happy to see their face when they look at the pictures I just took of them.

What's the worst or most challenging part of your job?

Overthinking what (if anything) I could have done differently.

What's the most surprising thing about your job?

I learn something new every day. Product technology is constantly changing, clients want subtle changes (a little risky but not too risky), and seeing my client's hair as they leave and wondering if I would change anything with her formula. I love when my clients return and tell me they love what I did the time before. That's my favorite part.

What kinds of qualities do you think one needs to be successful at this job?

1. Be a good listener.
2. Ask questions.
3. Remember your clients' birthdays.
4. Communicate cost for services.
5. Be reliable, always.

How do you combat burnout?

Practice self-care. This is so important. Rest, read, get some exercise. Listen to music that helps uplift you. Have another artistic outlet besides hair to keep your artistic flow—fluid. I highly recommend these books to help you in this process:

1. *Big Magic* by Elizabeth Gilbert
2. *The Artist's Way* by Julia Cameron
3. *The War of Art* by Steven Pressfield

What would you tell a young person who is thinking about becoming a hairstylist?

Keep learning. Find the best and upcoming leaders in the industry. Follow them on social media. Watch their feeds and videos on consultations, approach, and processing. Take classes and practice. Don't take anything personally, and understand the value of constructive criticism; it only makes you better. As a hair artist, I'm given the task of helping my clients authenticate the impression they leave with others. I want my clients' truest, most powerful self to set the tone in their various environments. I love that my clients can share their confidences and insecurities, so that together we can bring forth confidently their best self. My greatest artistic mentor, Hillary Clifton, took me under her wing and guided me to trust what I was feeling artistically and how to listen/communicate with my clients during our consultation. We must understand the unwritten/unspoken conditions that come with honing our skills. Disappointment, fear, artistic block, discouragement, and criticism are simply teachers. The only way to make the most of honing your craft is to welcome these frequent visitors and keep putting one foot in front of the other. Each new day will offer the opportunity to press on, and persevere we must. My goal with every client (new or established) is to play a small part in their everyday people seeing them differently. That is the heart and soul of what it is that I do.

Summary

This chapter covered aspects of college and post-secondary schooling that you'll want to consider as you move forward. Remember that finding the right fit is especially important as it increases the chances that you'll stay in school and earn your qualification or degree as well as have an amazing experience while you're at it.

In this chapter, we discussed how to evaluate and compare your options in order to get the best education for the lowest cost. You also learned a little about scholarships and financial aid, how the SAT and ACT tests work, and how to write a unique personal statement that eloquently expresses your passions.

Use this chapter as a jumping-off point to dig deeper into your particular area of interest. Some tidbits of wisdom to leave you with:

- Take the SAT and ACT tests early in your junior year so you have time to take them again. Most universities will automatically accept your highest score. Not all community colleges require that you take these tests.

- Make sure that the institution you plan to attend has an accredited program in your field of study. Some professions follow national accreditation policies while others are state-mandated and therefore differ across state lines. Do your research and understand the differences.

- Don't underestimate how important school visits are, especially in the pursuit of finding the right academic fit. Go prepared to ask questions not addressed on that school's website or in the literature.

- Your personal statement is a very important part of your application that can set you apart from others. Take the time and energy needed to make it unique and compelling.

- Don't assume you can't afford a school based on the "sticker price." Many schools offer great scholarships and aid to qualified students. It doesn't hurt to apply. This advice especially applies to minorities, veterans, and students with disabilities.

- Don't lose sight of the fact that it's important to pursue a career that you enjoy, are good at, and are passionate about! You'll be a happier person if you do so.

At this point, your career goals and aspirations should be gelling. At the least, you should have a plan for finding out more information. Remember to do the research on any college or school program that interests you before you reach out and especially before you visit. Faculty and staff find students who ask challenging questions much more impressive than those who ask questions that can be answered by spending ten minutes on the school website.

In chapter 4, we go into detail about the next steps: writing a resume and cover letter, interviewing well, being effective in follow-up communications, and more. This is information you can use to secure internships, volunteer positions, summer jobs, and more. It's not just for college grads. In fact, the sooner you hone these communication skills, the better off you'll be in the professional world.

4

Writing Your Resume and Interviewing

You are now well on your way to mapping your path to achieve your career goals in the cosmetology field. With each chapter of this book, we have narrowed the process from the broadest of strokes—what is the cosmetology and beauty industry and what kinds of jobs exist in it—to how to plan your strategy and educational approach to making your dream job a reality.

In this chapter, we will cover the steps involved in applying for jobs or to schools: how to prepare an effective resume and slam dunk an interview. Your resume is your opportunity to summarize your experience, training, education, and goals and attract employers or school administrators when applying for a job or to cosmetology programs or other degree programs. The goal of a resume is to land an interview, and the goal of an interview is to land a job or admission to a program. Even if you do not have much working experience, you can still put together a resume that expresses your interests and goals and the activities that illustrate your competence and interest.

As well as a resume, you will be expected to write a cover letter. This is basically your opportunity to reveal a little bit more about your passion and your motivation for a particular job or educational opportunity, and it's a chance to give a potential employer a sense of who you are personally and what drives you. And particularly because you are striving for a career in a very competitive and creative field, it's wise to ensure your uniqueness, creative flair, and passion for providing and learning about beauty care–related services comes through.

Giving the right impression is undoubtedly important, but don't let that make you nervous. In a resume, cover letter, or interview, you want to put forward your best but your genuine self. Dress professionally, proofread carefully, and ensure you are being yourself. In this chapter, we will cover all of these important aspects of the job-hunting process, and by the end, you will feel confident and ready to present yourself as a candidate for the job you really want.

TIP: For a job in a creative field such as cosmetology, it's important to be able to showcase your talents by sharing some of your results. Be sure and put together a photo portfolio of your strongest looks and styles. This can be created online for easier sharing and updating. See chapter 2, and look into free online website-building tools such as WordPress and Wix.

Writing Your Resume

Writing your first resume can be very challenging because you have likely not yet gained a lot of experience in a professional setting. But don't fret: employers and administrators understand that you are new to the workforce or to the particular career you are seeking. The right approach is never to exaggerate or invent experience or accomplishments but to present yourself as someone with a good work ethic and a genuine interest in the particular job or program and then to use what you can to present yourself authentically and honestly.

There are some standard elements in an effective resume that you should be sure to include. At the top should be your name, of course, as well as email address and other contact information. Always list your experience in chronological order, beginning with your current or most recent position—or whatever experience you want to share. If you are a recent graduate with little work experience, begin with your education. If you've been in the working world for a while, you can opt to list your education or any certifications you have at the end. The important thing is to present the most important and relevant information at the top. Your resume needs to be easy to navigate and read.

But before you even begin to write your resume, do your research. Make sure you have a good sense of what kind of candidate or applicant the school or employer is looking for. You want to not only come across as competent and qualified, you want to show that you're just the right fit for just that job within that organization.

Once you know more about the intended audience—organization, institution, or individual—of your resume, you can begin to make a list of all the relevant experience and education you have. You may need to customize your resume for different purposes to ensure you are not filling it with information that does not directly relate to your qualifications for a particular job or program.

Highlight your education where you can—any courses you've taken, be it in high school or through a community college or any other place that offers training related to your job or program target. Also highlight any hobbies or volunteer experience you have—but again, only as it relates to the position you are after.

"There are many diverse personalities in my chair so I make it a point to make them feel they are my only focus. I give them undivided attention and try and stay current with news, pop culture, movies, and music. It can be awkward when there is just silence unless you can read the person and get the feeling they would rather not engage. Other than that, let your personality do the work, but keep it professional."—Michelle Hatch, haistylist

Your resume is a document that sums up who you are and indicates in what ways you will be an asset to your future employer or program. But the trick is it should also be concise: one page is usually appropriate, especially for your very first resume.

TIP: Before preparing your resume, try to connect with a hiring professional—a human resources person or hiring manager—in a similar position or place of business you are interested in. They can give you advice on what employers and administrators look for and what information to highlight on your resume as well as what types of interview questions you can expect.

As important as your resume's content is the way you design and format it. You can find samples online of resumes that you can be inspired by. At the Balance Careers,[1] for example, you can find many templates and design ideas. You want your resume to be attractive to the eye and formatted in a way that makes the key points easy to spot and digest. According to research, employers take an average of six seconds to review a resume so you don't have a lot of time to get across your experience and value.

Linking-In with Impact

As well as your paper or electronic resume, creating a LinkedIn profile is a good way to highlight your experience and promote yourself as well as to network. Joining professional organizations or connecting with other people in your desired field are good ways to keep abreast of changes and trends and work opportunities.

The key elements of a LinkedIn profile are your photo, your headline, and your profile summary. These are the most revealing parts of the profile and the ones employers and connections will base their impression of you on.

The photo should be carefully chosen. Remember that LinkedIn is not Facebook or Instagram: it is not the place to share a photo of you on vacation or at a party. According to Joshua Waldman, author of *Job Searching with Social Media for Dummies*,[2] the choice of photo should be taken seriously and be done right. His tips:

- Choose a photo in which you have a nice smile.
- Dress in professional clothing.
- Ensure the background of the photo is pleasing to the eye. (According to Waldman, some colors—like green and blue—convey a feeling of trust and stability.)
- Remember it's not a mug shot. You can be creative with the angle of your photo rather than staring directly into the camera.
- Use your photo to convey some aspect of your personality.
- Focus on your face. Remember that visitors to your profile will see only a small thumbnail image so be sure your face takes up most of it.

"We must understand the unwritten/unspoken conditions that come with honing our skills. Disappointment, fear, artistic block, discouragement, and criticism are simply teachers. The only way to make the most of honing your craft is to welcome these frequent visitors and keep putting one foot in front of the other."—Taj Maxedon, hairstylist

Your headline will appear just below your name and should summarize—in 120 characters—who you are, what you do, what you are interested in doing, and what you are motivated by. Take your time with this—it is your opportunity to sell yourself in a brief and impactful manner. Related but separate is your summary section. Here you can share a little more about yourself than in your headline, but it should still be brief. Waldman recommends your summary take no more than thirty seconds to read aloud (so yes, time yourself!) and that it be short (between five and ten lines or three to five sentences), concise, and unique. It should tell a story.

Writing Your Cover Letter

As well as your resume, most employers will ask that you submit a cover letter. This is a one-page letter in which you express your motivation, why you are interested in the organization or position, and what skills you possess that make you the right fit.

Here are some tips for writing an effective cover letter.

- As always, proofread your text carefully before submitting it.
- Be sure the letter is focused on the specific job or program. Do not make it too general or one-size-fits-all.
- Summarize why you are right for the position.
- Keep your letter to one page.
- Introduce yourself in a way that makes the reader want to know more about you and encourages them to review your resume.
- Be specific about the job you are applying for. Mention the title and be sure it is correct.
- Try to find the name of the person who will receive your letter rather than keeping it non-specific ("To whom it may concern").
- Be sure you include your contact info.
- End with a "call to action"—a request for an interview, for example.

SEEING THE WORLD AND DISCOVERING ENTREPRENEURIAL POTENTIAL

Adam Tullett began his hairdressing career at the age of fourteen in his native England. Now the owner of a Toni&Guy salon in Haarlem, the Netherlands, through his career he has been able to apply his passion for art, hair, and people as well as have the opportunity to travel the world with a job he loves.

Adam Tullett. ADAM TULLETT.

Why did you choose to become a hairdresser and later run your own business?

I began hairdressing in 2003, at the age of fourteen. I always had an affinity with hair but couldn't explain exactly what it was that made me turn up for the interview other than my mum had an appointment at Toni&Guy and came back with an offer. When I walked into the salon, the atmosphere was incredible. All the staff were stylish and confident and glowing with passion. I knew then and there, "Wow this is for me." I found out that Toni&Guy was a global franchise group, and I had always wanted to see the world. This was my opportunity. I loved to make an impression on people from a young age, make people laugh and smile, and I was drawing and painted constantly. Now I can do this on people's heads!

What was the biggest challenge when you first transitioned to running your own salon?

Launching a business isn't for the fainthearted. I had studied all aspects of hairdressing and managed hairdressers and people for other salon owners before, but this, however, was a whole new ball game. I bought an existing franchise, with limited staffing and even fewer clients. It was starting a new business in a worn-out business. I had no capital and had to make it work to pay the bills so I worked my hands to the bone six days a week for almost two years. I hired new young talent to help me grow. Still growing, to be continued.

What is a typical day on the job for you?

A typical day in my job is coaching the staff, guiding the young talent, and looking after the clients' needs. Making people look and feel beautiful. One of the biggest missions we have is to first consult and diagnose, then advise what is best to do with the hair the client has and their requirements. A successful communication is key to a successful end result—perception is a funny thing. With good communication, you can perceive and achieve the same goal.

What's the best part of your job?

The best part of my job by far is to grow new, fresh young hairdressers. I love giving people the opportunities and drive I was presented with as a young hairdresser. And I love to see people's skill set blossom.

What's the worst or most challenging part of your job?

I have to say it's not all roses. I hate the cleaning and the itchy hairs all in my clothes. It's worth it, though.

What's the most surprising thing about your job?

The biggest surprise about being a salon owner is there isn't a day that goes by that you don't learn something new about coaching employees. They can always surprise you with a different angle or view on something. For example, how to improve customer service. They can show you different perspectives that you don't see as the owner. I love being continually challenged and learning all the time.

What do you see as your next career step?

I will 100 percent be slowing down the hairdresser role in the near future to make space for the younger hairdressers and become more of the entrepreneur I wish to be. But I absolutely love it with everything I have. From here, I intend to open a couple more franchises and maybe dive into some other industries too. I love fashion and would love a clothing store and maybe a bar one day too.

Interviewing Skills

With your sparkling resume and LinkedIn profile, you are bound to be called for an interview. This is an important stage to reach: you will have already gone through several filters—a potential employer or administrator has gotten a quick scan of your experience and has reviewed your LinkedIn profile and has made the decision to learn more about you in person.

Regardless of the type of position or job you are seeking in the cosmetology industry—from eyebrow waxer to hair color specialist—you will inevitably have to face the somewhat daunting experience known as the job interview. You will find yourself face-to-face with the person you are tasked with convincing to hire you. No pressure, right? A person you've likely never met before will, in a relatively short time, decide whether you are right for a coveted job in their salon or beauty business.

Everyone will likely tell you to be yourself, be confident, be calm. That's easier said than done—but don't fret. Even though you probably won't know the person or people you will interview with or the specific questions you will be asked (or, more important, the answers they want to hear), there are ways to prepare ahead of time. And doing so will help you arrive at calmness and confidence.

In any job interview, there are certain questions you can anticipate being asked. They are fairly standard regardless of the position for which you are applying or indeed the field in which you want to work. Cosmetologist Life,[3] a site that provides, in its own words, "career advice for hairstylists," has generously offered a list of questions you will almost certainly be asked in a hairdresser job interview (which also apply to other areas of cosmetology) and the types of answers that will help you nail the interview and earn yourself an offer. What follows are the top-ten questions and recommended types of answers. For the rest of the list, visit the site. It never hurts to be prepared.

1. Tell Me About Yourself.

This one may sound like an easy question, but it's a bit of a trick. Although your personality is important in the cosmetology field—and indeed wherever you work, your potential boss and colleagues will want to get a sense of what it would be like to work with you each day and whether there's a personality "click"—what this question is actually intended to reveal is in what ways you will benefit the salon or place of business.

Cosmetologist Life calls this your "unique selling point," or USP, and suggests an answer such as "I am a very quick study and use my free time to further my skills and research hair techniques. I am great with time management, have a lot of customer service experience and a strong work ethic. I am passionate about all things hair but my true love is in hairstyling and updos."

2. Do you consider yourself a team player?

Teamwork is key in a salon. Even if you honestly know yourself *not* to be a team player, understand that this is a key characteristic for succeeding in the cosmetology business. Cosmetologist Life advises you rather bluntly to work on becoming a team player, and, they write, "If this question is asked and you are *not* a team player, meaning you prefer to work alone, fake it." Being self-absorbed will quickly disqualify you.

3. Why do you want to work for us?

This question is designed to understand and be convinced by your motivation. Are you passionate about the company, the job, or do you just need a paycheck? It's important to convey not only commitment and enthusiasm for the type of work you would be doing but also for the particular business you are applying to.

Do your research. Be able to comment on the salon, what you like about its culture, for example, or its training opportunities or the special services it provides. Be positive about the business and be able to articulate how you would be an asset to the current culture.

Here's a sample answer offered by Cosmetologist Life: "La Bella Foo Foo Salon has an outstanding reputation for customer service and beautiful color services. I love doing color more than anything and intend on becoming a master colorist within two years. I can't think of anywhere I would rather begin my beauty career and learn from the best."

4. Why should we hire you?

Perhaps it goes against your constitution if you are not used to being confident to the point of actually bragging, but now is not the time to be humble. You want to answer this one confidently and assuredly—and also briefly—so they feel sure that you are sure of yourself and your abilities and the contributions you will undoubtedly bring to their place of business.

Cosmetologist Life suggests this type of answer: "Because I have a strong work ethic, I'm great at time management, I understand the importance of superior customer service, and I am willing to do everything I can to help the salon and myself grow." And if you're confident enough to say something like "Because I will exceed your expectations," go for it—but have a convincing supporting statement to back it up.

5. What did you like best about your last job?

Your answer to this question will give the interviewer a sense of your focus on the job. If you say you loved the people you worked with, it shows you are a team player who gets along well with coworkers. You can also focus on customer service ("I love making customers happy!") or the variety of the work ("I loved the challenge of working on various aspects of beauty services, from skin care to nail care"). Or maybe there were many professional development opportunities in your last job.

If this is your first professional job interview, resort to your training, and talk about what you liked most about your cosmetology school experience.

6. What did you like least about your last job?

Be careful here. Even if the truth is you couldn't stand your manager or coworkers or you didn't like the hours you had to work, keep your answer here positive. It may seem like an invitation to complain or vent, but it is definitely not.

Focus on something that enhances something positive about you. Perhaps your last job wasn't even in the cosmetology industry, in which case it's a no-brainer to say you want to find a job doing what you have trained for and love. Or perhaps there were no growth opportunities in your last job. That's a valid answer that shows you are ready and eager to be challenged in your career.

7. What was the best job you ever had? Why?

For this answer, definitely tie it to something you will be expected to be doing in the salon to which you are applying. If you loved guiding music class during a kids' summer camp or preparing pizzas at the local pizzeria, that will not really be very relevant to a cosmetology career.

Even if you have never worked in a salon, you can find a way to talk about an aspect of a job you've held that relates. Customer service, creativity, team work, continuous learning opportunities, a high level of movement versus sitting at a desk—these are work experiences and skills that you will use in a cosmetology career.

8. What was the worst job you ever had? Why?

Be mindful of this one too: again, it's a bit of a trap. Just as with question 6 earlier, this is not your license to complain or speak negatively about a previous job. Find an answer that sounds like a viable reason why another job wasn't for you but in doing so emphasizes how a job in this particular salon *is* for you. A good answer would be "I worked as a receptionist, but I found it a bit dull that I didn't interact with people face-to-face and that I had to stay put at my desk all day."

Avoid strong words like "hate." Talk about something not being a good fit, for example, to keep from sounding too negative or emotional.

9. What are your greatest strengths?

This is another question that calls on you to be confident and self-assured. Sell yourself! Let them know exactly what you've got and why you are the person they need to hire for the position. Let your best skills shine—but again, keep it relevant (they don't really care if you're a very good driver or score high points in your favorite computer game). An example of a good answer, according to Cosmetologist Life, would be "I am a hard worker, highly efficient, and am able to maintain a positive attitude. I'm also very passionate about hair and am excited to start my beauty career."

10. What is your greatest weakness?

This is probably the least liked, most dreaded question of all interview time. Who is going to admit they have a hard time remembering things or that they often oversleep? Definitely don't tell them something like that (and definitely resolve these issues if they are true!). Instead, as with other such "trick" questions, turn a negative into a positive.

Choose something that won't directly impact your performance, reliability, or skill set in your work—which, of course, would in turn negatively affect the business. Talk in general terms. Cosmetologist Life suggests, "Don't choose anything that could adversely affect salon life. Things like being too trusting, or being too guarded with your feelings, or taking on too much responsibility are good ones to use that won't work against you. Whatever you choose, make sure to add 'But I'm working on it.'"

There's no way to know ahead of time exactly what to expect in an interview, but there are many ways to prepare yourself. You can start by learning more about the person who will be interviewing you. In the same way recruiters and employers can learn about you online, you can do the same. You can see if you have any education or work experience in common or any contacts you both know.

A job interview can be stressful, naturally. You can help calm your nerves and feel more confident if you prepare ahead by thinking about answers to questions you can anticipate being asked. GETTY IMAGES/SDI PRODUCTIONS.

Preparing yourself for the types of questions you will be asked to ensure you offer a thoughtful and meaningful response is vital to interview success. Consider your answers carefully and be prepared to support them with examples and anecdotes. Here are examples of more questions.

- Why did you decide enter this field? What drives your passion for cosmetology?
- What is your educational background? What credentials did you earn?
- What did you like best about the educational experience? What did you like least?
- Where and how were you trained?
- What is your management style? What management style do you want your supervisor to have?
- Do employees report to you? How many? What level are the employees who are your direct reports?

- Describe your usual role in a team-centered work environment. Do you easily assume a leadership role?

BEWARE WHAT YOU SHARE ON SOCIAL MEDIA

Most of us engage in social media. Sites such as Facebook, Twitter, and Instagram give us a platform for sharing photos and memories, opinions and life events, and allow us to reveal everything from our political stance to our sense of humor. It's a great way to connect with people around the world, but once you post something, it's accessible to anyone—including potential employers—unless you take mindful precautions.

Your posts may be public, which means you may be making the wrong impression without realizing it. More and more, people are using search engines like Google to get a sense of potential employers, colleagues, or employees, and the impression you make online can have a strong impact on how you are perceived. According to CareerBuilder,[4] 60 percent of employers search for information on candidates on social media sites.

Glassdoor[5] offers the following tips to keep your social media activity from sabotaging your career success.

- Check your privacy settings. Ensure that your photos and posts are only accessible to the friends or contacts you want to see them. You want to come across as professional and reliable.
- Rather than avoid social media while searching for a job, use it to your advantage. Give future employees a sense of your professional interests by liking pages or joining professional organizations related to your career goals.
- Be attentive to the quality of writing of all your posts and comments. Grammar counts.
- Be consistent. With each social media outlet, there is a different focus and tone to what you are communicating. LinkedIn is very professional while Facebook is far more social and relaxed. It's okay to take a different tone on various social media sites, but be sure you aren't blatantly contradicting yourself.
- Choose your username carefully. Remember, social media may be the first impression anyone has of you in the professional realm.

DRESSING APPROPRIATELY

How you dress for a job interview is very important to the impression you want to make. Remember that the interview, no matter what the actual environment in which you'd be working, is your chance to present your most professional self. Although you will not likely ever wear a suit to work, for an interview it's the most professional choice.

TIP: Although you may be applying for a job in a casual, laid-back environment, it's important to come across as a professional by dressing the part when you interview. If you are applying for a job in the beauty industry, personal hygiene will be particularly important. Be sure your nails are clean and well manicured, for example. Let your style shine through but keep it professional. If you wear makeup, keep it neutral. A suit may not be an absolute requirement, but avoid looking too casual as it will give the impression you are not that interested.

WHAT EMPLOYERS EXPECT

Hiring managers and human resources professionals will also have certain expectations of you at an interview. The main thing is preparation: it cannot be overstated that you should arrive at an interview appropriately dressed, on time, unhurried, and ready to answer—and ask—questions.

For any job interview, the main things employers will look for are that you

- have a thorough understanding of the organization and the job for which you are applying
- are prepared to answer questions about yourself and your relevant experience
- are poised and likeable but still professional. They will be looking for a sense of what it would be like to work with you on a daily basis and how your presence would fit in the culture of the business.
- stay engaged. Listen carefully to what is being asked and offer thoughtful but concise answers. Don't blurt out answers you've memorized but really focus on what is being asked.

- are prepared to ask your own questions. It shows how much you understand the flow of an organization or workplace and how you will contribute to it. Here are some questions you can ask:
  - ○ What created the need to fill this position? Is it a new position or has someone left the company?
  - ○ Where does this position fit in the overall hierarchy of the organization?
  - ○ What are the key skills required to succeed in this job?
  - ○ What challenges might I expect to face within the first six months on the job?
  - ○ How does this position relate to the achievement of the company's goals?
  - ○ How would you describe the company culture?

THE JOY OF SEEING CONFIDENCE RADIATE IN CLIENTS

Bryhannon Natale is a native Arizonan who now lives in Miami, Florida. She is the owner of Nude Wax Company in Miami Springs, Florida, and recently celebrated three years in business. She enjoys cooking and spending time outdoors while focusing on raising her children to be exceptional and kind humans to others as well as to our planet. As a waxing professional, she currently holds an esthetic license in Arizona and Florida.

Why did you choose to become an esthetician, specializing in waxing?

Before I became an esthetician, I really liked the results of waxing. Once I started school, I was

Bryhannon Natale. BRYHANNON NATALE.

waxing my whole body at that point because we all needed the practice. I fell in love. Waxing results last much longer than shaving and I experienced so much less skin irritation than when I would shave. I think personally loving the services you offer makes it much easier to get people on board with why they would love it too! Another reason that I picked specializing in waxing, out of all the different services estheticians are licensed to do, was because the results are instant. Many people are instant gratification oriented. To be able to come in super fuzzy and leave smooth and confident, well, I'm not sure anything beats that! There is no wait! Although an added, long-term perk to consistent waxing is that over time the hair thins out drastically. That makes for a quicker, less painful wax and longer lasting results.

What is a typical day on the job for you?

I currently wear all the hats in my business. A typical waxing day starts with getting to the salon earlier than I need to be there just to start my morning a little slower. Getting fresh juice from the bakery next door is my "morning coffee." I wait to turn the lights on and let that natural light from the windows stream in. I turn on my favorite Pandora station, Sam Smith. Next, I start melting down wax and get ready for the fifteen to twenty-five clients that I typically see per day. My hours vary. I have a couple of days a week when I stay late for the clients needing an appointment after work. Appointments, at my salon, are booked back to back, which is how I work best, although I did finally start blocking out time for a lunch break! (I strongly recommend this!) I have my timing down very well and have a strict late policy that actually benefits my clients by allowing them to really count on me for what time they will be in and out. I schedule more time for first-time clients so that I have a little time to chat with them and answer any questions! After I am done with all of my clients, I return any phone calls and clean up, to leave it ready for the next day. I run a daily report and write any notes for myself if I have any pending tasks for the following day. I set specific office days for myself since this is a typical wax day for me. Office days are mostly spent at the salon while occasionally they are at home. Office days include keeping up with all reporting, licensing, and so on as well as inventory, scheduling, innovative planning, social media, marketing, and much more.

What's the best part of your job?

The best part of my job is, by far, the confidence that radiates from my clients when their services are done. Even if they waxed an area no one sees, they hold their head higher and have that mentality of *I can do anything!* I love being a part of that.

What's the worst or most challenging part of your job?

The most challenging part of my job is wearing all the hats! The busier I was waxing, the less I was able to engage on social media, think of new ideas and better ways to work. That is the hard part! For this reason, I ended up making office days or hours. These times are dedicated solely to engagement and behind-the-scenes business tasks! If you are not hiring someone to do those jobs, you will need to do them yourself, and do them well, to be successful.

What's the most surprising thing about your job?

The most surprising thing about my job has been the overwhelming kindness, love, and continued support my clients have shown me. They have all been there to cheer me on at every milestone. I was thinking this job would entail just me doing services for them, but in return they do so much for me! That also made word of mouth a huge component in helping me grow my client base exponentially through these three years.

What kinds of qualities do you think one needs to be successful at this job?

ambitious
communicative
dedicated
adaptable
patient (with yourself and others)

How do you combat burnout?

I was the queen of burning myself out! I thought that showed how dedicated you are and how hard you work. Which it can, but not in the best way. For me, the way I was able to combat this was reconstructing my schedule in a way that was more conducive to all the tasks that I needed to accomplish—as well as being human. I started with giving myself a lunch break. Sounds silly, right? Well, it changed the game for me. It had a positive, rippling effect throughout my day. I was able to slow down for a moment after being back-to-back all morning. I was able to eat—that's just necessary as a human. I was able to restock my room—without rushing. I even managed to return phone calls! This was a good way to see I was already half done with my day too! Once I reached the end of my day, I usually had few to no calls left to return, my room needed less restocking, and I wasn't starving! So give yourself a lunch break because thirty to forty-five minutes midday goes a long way! The next thing I did was dedicate days (or hours) to just business. This also impacted my efficiency greatly. Instead of trying to do important tasks in pieces between clients, if I had fifteen minutes, I was able to complete things start to finish. This also keeps things pretty fresh because days on end of the same thing in any capacity can be draining.

What would you tell a young person who is thinking about becoming an esthetician?

I would tell any young person who is considering becoming an esthetician, or waxer, to make sure what you are doing lights a fire inside of you. As I mentioned, personally loving what you do can make it so much easier to get people on board with why they might love it too. Do all the research you can, and when you think you've done it all—do even more. Read books about your industry. In the beauty industry, perhaps more than any other, you will need to constantly be in the know. Trends are always changing, colors too. There are often newer techniques, and there are *always* new products. You need to stand out. You need to be able to explain and show what makes you different from any other service provider that provides that same service. Be authentically yourself. Be fluid and adaptable, as the world is ever-changing. Surround yourself with supporters and people that believe you can do this . . . because you can.

Summary

Congratulations on working through the book! You should now have a strong idea of your career goals within the cosmetology and beauty industry and how to realize them. In this chapter, we covered how to present yourself as the right candidate to a potential employer or administrator—and these strategies are also relevant if you are applying to a college or another form of training.

Here are some tips to sum it up.

- Your resume should be concise, and it should be focused on only relevant aspects of your work experience or education. Although you can include personal hobbies or details, they should be related to the job and your qualifications for it.
- Take your time with all your professional documents—your resume, your cover letter, your LinkedIn profile—and be sure to proofread very carefully to avoid embarrassing and sloppy mistakes.
- Prepare yourself for an interview by anticipating the types of questions you will be asked and coming up with professional and meaningful responses.
- Equally, prepare some questions to ask your potential employer at the interview. This will show you have a good understanding and interest in the organization and what role you would have in it.
- Always follow up an interview with a letter or an email. An email is the fastest way to express your gratitude for the interviewer's time and to restate your interest in the position.
- Dress appropriately for the interview and pay extra attention to tidiness and hygiene.

- Be wary of what you share on social media sites while job searching. Most employers research candidates online, and what you have shared will influence their idea of who you are and what it would be like to work with you.

The beauty industry is an exciting one with many different types of jobs and work environments. This book has described the various jobs and provided examples of real, working professionals and their impressions of what they do and how they prepared—through education or training—to do it. We hope this will further inspire you to identify your goal and know how to achieve it.

You've chosen a field that is expected to grow in the coming years and one that will offer a creative, diverse, competitive, exciting career path. People will always be interested in looking and feeling their best, and the demand for beauty care and treatment will never disappear—in fact, it seems to only increase. We wish you great success in your future.

Notes

Introduction

1. U.S. Bureau of Labor Statistics, "Barbers, Hairstylists, and Cosmetologists," www.bls.gov/ooh/media-and-communication/broadcast-and-sound-engineering -technicians.htm.

2. U.S. Bureau of Labor Statistics, "Barbers, Hairstylists, and Cosmetologists: Job Outlook," www.bls.gov/ooh/personal-care-and-service/barbers-hairstylists-and -cosmetologists.htm#tab-6.

3. USAWage.com, "Highest-paying Cities for Hairdressers, Hairstylists, and Cosmetologists," www.usawage.com/high-pay/cities-hairdressers_hairstylists_and _cosmetologists.php.

4. U.S. Bureau of Labor Statistics, "Skincare Specialists," www.bls.gov/ooh/ personal-care-and-service/skincare-specialists.htm.

Chapter 1

1. Douglas Harper, "cosmetology (n.)," Online Etymology Dictionary, www .etymonline.com/word/cosmetology.

2. Bethany Biron, "Beauty Has Blown Up to Be a $532 Billion Industry—And Analysts Say That These 4 Trends Will Make It Even Bigger," *Business Insider*, July 9, 2019, www.businessinsider.com/beauty-multibillion-industry-trends-future-2019 -7?international=true&r=US&IR=T.

3. Ljubica Cvetkovska, "45 Beauty Statistics That Will Impress You," Loud CloudHealth.com, https://loudcloudhealth.com/beauty-industry-statistics/.

4. Mintel, "Salon Services, US, June 2012," https://store.mintel.com/ salon-services-us-june-2012.

5. Athena Jones, "Hair Salons and Barbershops: A Growing Industry," CNN, October 15, 2011, https://edition.cnn.com/2011/10/15/us/hair-salons -economy/?hpt=us_t2.

6. *U.S. News & World Report*, "Best Social Service Jobs," https://money.usnews.com/careers/best-jobs/hairdresser?PageNr=1.

7. Salon Success Academy, "Proof the Beauty Industry Is Recession-Proof," July 9, 2011, www.salonsuccessacademy.com/blog/proof-that-the-beauty-industry-is-recession-proof/.

8. April Long, "The History of Beauty," *Elle*, January 25, 2010, www.elle.com/beauty/makeup-skin-care/tips/a12060/the-history-of-beauty-392834/.

9. Bureau of Labor Statistics, "Focusing on Style: Careers in Personal Appearance," www.bls.gov/careeroutlook/2018/article/personal-appearance-workers.htm.

10. Bureau of Labor Statistics, "Barbers, Hairstylists, and Cosmetologists," www.bls.gov/ooh/personal-care-and-service/barbers-hairstylists-and-cosmetologists.htm.

11. Bureau of Labor Statistics, "Manicurists and Pedicurists," www.bls.gov/ooh/personal-care-and-service/manicurists-and-pedicurists.htm.

12. Payscale.com, "Average Beautician Hourly Pay," www.payscale.com/research/US/Job=Beautician/Hourly_Rate.

13. Payscale.com, "Average Wedding Stylist Hourly Pay," www.payscale.com/research/US/Job=Wedding_Stylist/Hourly_Rate.

14. Payscale.com, "Average Makeup Artist Hourly Pay," www.payscale.com/research/US/Job=Makeup_Artist/Hourly_Rate.

15. Bureau of Labor Statistics, "Skincare Specialists," www.bls.gov/ooh/personal-care-and-service/skincare-specialists.htm.

Chapter 2

1. FreeAdvice, "Franchises," https://business-law.freeadvice.com/business-law/franchise_law/.

Chapter 3

1. Stephen R. Antonoff, MD, "College Personality Quiz," *U.S. News & World Report*, July 31, 2018, www.usnews.com/education/best-colleges/right-school/choices/articles/college-personality-quiz.

2. TheBestSchools.org, "The 50 Best Community Colleges in the United States," February 3, 2020, https://thebestschools.org/50-community-colleges-united-states/.

3. U.S. Department of Education, "Complete the FAFSA Form," Federal Student Aid, https://studentaid.gov/h/apply-for-aid/fafsa.

Chapter 4

1. Dotdash, "Student Resume Examples, Templates, and Writing Tips," The Balance Careers, www.thebalancecareers.com/student-resume-examples-and-templates -2063555.

2. Joshua Waldman, *Job Searching with Social Media for Dummies* (Hoboken, NJ: Wiley & Sons, 2013).

3. cosmetolgistlife.com, "Your New Beauty Career: The Top Interview Questions & How to Breeze Right Through Them," www.cosmetologistlife.com/Beauty -Career-Interview-Questions.html.

4. CareerBuilder, Newsroom, www.careerbuilder.com/share/aboutus/press releasesdetail.aspx?ed=12%2F31%2F2016&id=pr945&sd=4%2F28%2F2016.

5. Alice E. M. Underwood, "9 Things to Avoid on Social Media While Looking for a New Job," Glassdoor, January 3, 2018, www.glassdoor.com/blog/things-to-avoid -on-social-media-job-search/.

Glossary

bachelor's degree: A four-year degree awarded by a college or university.

beautician: A professional in the cosmetology industry.

burnout: A feeling of physical or emotional exhaustion caused by overwork.

campus: The location of a school, college, or university.

career assessment test: A test that asks questions geared to identify the test taker's skills and interests to help inform the test taker on what type of career would suit them.

colleagues: The people an employee works with.

community college: A two-year college that awards associate's degrees.

cosmetology: The art or profession of applying makeup, styling and treating hair, and performing other beauty treatments.

cosmetology school: An institution that focuses on the study of cosmetology by preparing graduates for a career in that field.

cover letter: A document that usually accompanies a resume and allows the candidate applying to a job or a school or internship an opportunity to describe his or her motivation and qualifications.

Criteria Basic Skills Test (CBST): A test measuring the basic math and verbal skills required to succeed in a wide variety of entry-level jobs.

Customer Service Aptitude Profile (CSAP): A test measuring the personality traits needed to be successful in a customer-service-oriented career.

educational background: The degrees a person has earned and the schools he or she has attended.

entrepreneur: A person who creates, launches, and manages his or her own business.

epilator: An electronic device used to remove unwanted hair by grabbing the hairs and pulling them out.

esthetician: A person who specializes in beautification of the skin.

financial aid: Various means of receiving financial support for the purpose of attending school. This can be a grant or a scholarship, for example.

franchise: The right granted (through purchase) to an individual to use the branding and market the products or services of a specific business.

freelancer: A person who owns their own business through which they provide services to a variety of clients.

General Educational Development (GED): A degree earned by non–high school graduates that is the equivalent of a high school diploma.

hairstylist: A person who cuts, colors, and styles hair as a profession.

internship: A work-experience opportunity that lasts a set period of time and can be paid or unpaid.

interpersonal skills: The ability to communicate and interact with other people in an effective manner.

interviewing: A part of the job-seeking process in which a candidate meets with a potential employer, usually face-to-face, in order to discuss the candidate's work experience and education and to allow the candidate to seek information about the position.

job market: A market in which employers search for employees and employees search for jobs.

laser hair removal: A means of hair removal that became popular in the United States in the 1990s. It is a process by which light is directed at unwanted hair, destroying the hair follicles. Though not permanent, it is much more effective than other methods in preventing hair from growing back.

major: The subject or course of study in which an individual chooses to earn his or her degree.

makeup artist: A person who specializes in applying makeup for professionals, such as actors and news anchors, and for individuals who want to look their best for a special event such as a wedding.

manicure: A cosmetic treatment of the fingernails, including trimming and polishing.

nail-care technician: A person who gives manicures.

networking: The process of building, strengthening, and maintaining professional relationships as a way to further one's career goals.

on-the-job training: A type of training in which the individual learns a job while performing the same job in a real-world environment.

pedicure: A cosmetic treatment of the toenails, including trimming and polishing.

portfolio: A representation of work, such as photos of hairstyles or applied makeup, created by the individual responsible for that work.

profit: The difference between the money spent providing a product or service and the money gained from that activity.

resume: A document, usually one page, that outlines a person's professional experience and education. It is designed to give potential employers a sense of a job candidate's qualifications.

skin-care specialist: A person who is trained in the care of the skin.

social media: Websites and applications that enable users to create and share content online for networking and social-sharing purposes. Examples include Facebook and Instagram.

sugaring: A process of hair removal that is similar to waxing, but instead of wax, a sticky paste is applied to the area of unwanted hair and then removed along with the hair by means of a porous strip.

tuition: The money an individual pays for his or her education.

tweezers: A tool used to pluck and remove hair. Tweezers are often used on eyebrows.

waxer: A person who is trained to remove unwanted body hair such as from the legs or armpits using hot wax.

work culture: A concept that defines the beliefs, philosophy, thought processes, and attitudes of employees in a particular organization.

Resources

The following websites, magazines, and organizations can help you further investigate and educate yourself on cosmetology-related topics, all of which will help you as you take the next steps in your career and throughout your professional life.

Professional Organizations

Professional Beauty Association (PBA)
www.probeauty.org
An organization that supports and connects professional stylists, makeup artists, manufacturers, distributors, freelancers, employees, salons, spas, suppliers, and beauty schools as well as students pursuing these careers.

American Association of Cosmetology Schools (AACS)
www.beautyschools.org
An American nonprofit association open to all privately owned schools of cosmetology arts and sciences. AACS currently has more than three hundred school owners as members.

International Salon/Spa Business Network (ISBN)
https://salonspanetwork.org
An organization that helps professionals network and access and share industry news and information. It acts as a powerful lobbyist representing professionals in Washington.

The American Board of Certified Hair Colorists
www.haircolorist.com
An organization with the goal of establishing a standard by which to judge competence in and to acknowledge the level of excellence achieved in hair color.

Associated Hair Professionals (AHP)

www.associatedhairprofessionals.com

A membership organization that provides comprehensive liability insurance and business-support resources for hairstylists and barbers.

International Association of Professions Career College (IAP College)

www.iapcollege.com

An organization that offers affordable, online certificate programs for students and working professionals.

International Make-up Association (IMA)

https://ima-make-up.com

An industry association for makeup artists and those who want to employ makeup artists.

Associated Skin Care Professionals

https://www.ascpskincare.com

An organization that supports the careers and education of skin-care professionals.

Magazines

Hairdressers Journal Interactive (HJI)

www.hji.co.uk

One of the best-known salon magazines for hairdressing trends and industry news.

The Beauty Consultant

www.beautyconsultantmagazine.com

A source of news, product information, fashion updates, and celebrity chit-chat for beauty professionals.

Journal of Cosmetic Science

https://library.scconline.org/journal-of-cosmetic-science

A publisher of scientific papers concerned with cosmetics, cosmetic products, fragrances, human-skin physiology, color physics, and so on.

Modern Salon

www.modernsalon.com

A magazine and online resource that helps cosmetology professionals choose products, services, and education for their businesses by providing step-by-step education and creative inspiration.

ASCP Skin Deep

www.ascpskincare.com

A magazine for estheticians that provides news on the latest trends, techniques, and products and on the industry as a whole.

DERMASCOPE Magazine

www.dermascope.com

The first professional skin-care journal published in the United States.

Bibliography

Antonoff, Steven R. "College Personality Quiz." *U.S. News & World Report*, May 15, 2019. www.usnews.com/education/best-colleges/right-school/choices/articles/college-personality-quiz.

Biron, Bethany. "Beauty Has Blown Up to Be a $532 Billion Industry—And Analysts Say That These 4 Trends Will Make It Even Bigger." *Business Insider*, July 9, 2019. www.businessinsider.com/beauty-multibillion-industry-trends-future-2019-7?international=true&r=US&IR=T.

cosmetolgistlife.com. "Your New Beauty Career: The Top Interview Questions & How to Breeze Right Through Them." www.cosmetologistlife.com/Beauty-Career-Interview-Questions.html.

Cvetkovska, Ljubica. "45 Beauty Statistics That Will Impress You." LoudCloud Health.com. https://loudcloudhealth.com/beauty-industry-statistics/.

Dotdash. "Student Resume Examples, Templates, and Writing Tips." The Balance Careers. www.thebalancecareers.com/student-resume-examples-and-templates-2063555.

FreeAdvice. "Franchises." https://business-law.freeadvice.com/business-law/franchise_law/.

Harper, Douglas. "cosmetology (n.)." Online Etymology Dictionary. www.etymonline.com/word/cosmetology.

Jones, Athena. "Hair Salons and Barbershops: A Growing Industry." CNN, October 15, 2011. https://edition.cnn.com/2011/10/15/us/hair-salons-economy/?hpt=us_t2.

Long, April. "The History of Beauty." *Elle*, January 25, 2010. www.elle.com/beauty/makeup-skin-care/tips/a12060/the-history-of-beauty-392834/.

Payscale.com. "Average Beautician Hourly Pay." www.payscale.com/research/US/Job=Beautician/Hourly_Rate.

———. "Average Makeup Artist Hourly Pay." www.payscale.com/research/US/Job=Makeup_Artist/Hourly_Rate.

———. "Average Wedding Stylist Hourly Pay." www.payscale.com/research/US/Job=Wedding_Stylist/Hourly_Rate.

Salon Success Academy. "Proof the Beauty Industry Is Recession-Proof," July 9, 2011. www.salonsuccessacademy.com/blog/proof-that-the-beauty-industry-is-recession-proof/.

TheBestSchools.org. "The 50 Best Community Colleges in the United States," February 3, 2020. https://thebestschools.org/50-community-colleges-united-states/.

U.S. Bureau of Labor Statistics. "Barbers, Hairstylists, and Cosmetologists." www.bls.gov/ooh/media-and-communication/broadcast-and-sound-engineering-technicians.htm.

———. "Barbers, Hairstylists, and Cosmetologists: Job Outlook." www.bls.gov/ooh/personal-care-and-service/barbers-hairstylists-and-cosmetologists.htm#tab-6.

———. "Focusing on Style: Careers in Personal Appearance." www.bls.gov/careeroutlook/2018/article/personal-appearance-workers.htm.

———. "Manicurists and Pedicurists." www.bls.gov/ooh/personal-care-and-service/manicurists-and-pedicurists.htm.

———. "Skincare Specialists." www.bls.gov/ooh/personal-care-and-service/skincare-specialists.htm.

U.S. News & World Report. "Best Social Service Jobs." https://money.usnews.com/careers/best-jobs/hairdresser?PageNr=1.

USAWage.com. "Highest-Paying Cities for Hairdressers, Hairstylists, and Cosmetologists." www.usawage.com/high-pay/cities-hairdressers_hairstylists_and_cosmetologists.php.

Waldman, Joshua. *Job Searching with Social Media for Dummies.* Hoboken, NJ: Wiley & Sons, 2013.

About the Author

Tracy Brown Hamilton is a writer, editor, and journalist based in the Netherlands. She has written several books on topics ranging from careers to the media and economics to pop culture. She lives with her husband and three children.

Editorial Board

Eric Evitts has been working with teens in the high school setting for twenty-three years. Most of his career has focused on helping teens, especially at-risk students, find and follow a career path of interest. He has developed curriculum for Frederick County Public Schools on anti-bullying and career development. He is currently a counselor at South Hagerstown High School.

Danielle Irving-Johnson, MA, EdS, is currently career services specialist at the American Counseling Association. She exercises her specialty in career counseling by providing career guidance, services, and resources designed to encourage and assist students and professionals in obtaining their educational, employment, and career goals while also promoting the importance of self-care, wellness, work-life balance, and burnout prevention. Danielle has also served as a mental health counselor and clinical intake assessor in community agency settings assisting diverse populations with various diagnoses.

Joyce Rhine Shull, BS, MS, is an active member of the Maryland Association of Community College's Career Affinity Group and the Maryland Career Development Association. She presently serves as an academic advisor in higher education and teaches professionalism in the workplace as an adjunct professor. Her experience also includes two decades of management and career education in vocational courses and seminars for high school students.

Lisa Adams Somerlot is president of the American College Counseling Association and also serves as director of counseling at the University of West Georgia. She has a PhD in counselor education from Auburn University, is a licensed professional counselor in Georgia, and is a nationally approved clinical supervisor. She is certified in Myers Briggs Type Indicator, Strong Interest Inventory, and Strengths Quest administration.